HOW TO RAISE
A DOCTOR

Wisdom from Parents Who Did It

HOW TO RAISE A DOCTOR

Wisdom from Parents Who Did It

BY DALE OKORODUDU, MD

Clovercroft Publishing

How to Raise a Doctor

©2018 by Dale Okorodudu

Published by Clovercroft Publishing, Franklin, Tennessee

Edited by Christy Callahan

Cover Design by Debbie Manning Sheppard

Interior Design by Suzanne Lawing

ISBN: 978-1-945507-99-1

Printed in the United States of America

To God
You are the greatest of all parents!

To Janai
*I couldn't ask for a better wife and mother
of my children. I love you.*

To Tony, Jace, and Mavyn
*I thank God that He let me be your daddy.
Mommy and I will give our all to raise you right!*

To Papa and MaDear
*Thank you for the sacrifices made and
for fighting for my success. I love you and
hope I've made you proud.*

To Anthony, Anthonette, and Daniel
*Thank you for being the world's best siblings.
You helped raise a little brother!*

My philosophy is simple. To equip the children, we must first equip the parents. Let's do that.

—DALE OKORODUDU, MD

CONTENTS

PART 1

The Right Perspective

1

THE ADVANTAGE

If you don't have a competitive advantage, don't compete.
—JACK WELCH

That's my son Jace on the cover. He wants to be a fireman, not a doctor like his daddy. He's an amazing kid, and I truly do mean that! Vibrant, jovial, and adventurous. The type of child that lights up an entire room. Jace's older brother, Tony, is five, and his little sister, Mavyn, is an infant. Even at their tender young ages, you've never met prouder parents than my wife, Janai, and me. Okay, so right about now you're probably thinking, "Wait a second, Dr. Dale's kids are still young. What can he tell me about raising a doctor?" That's a fair question. Stick with me and I'll make it worth your while.

Tony was born in Durham, North Carolina, aka the City of Medicine. At the time, I was a resident physician at Duke University Medical Center. As you can imagine, with both parents being doctors, prophecies pertaining to his profession in medicine began when he was still in the womb. "Dr. Tony

Okorodudu! Future doctor! Scientist in the making! Surgeon General!" Society immediately designated him a success, simply because of who his parents were. Before my baby boy could even suck his own thumb, the bar had been set high for him. Actually, the bar had been set for his mother and me. We were expected to present a leader by the name of Tony Okorodudu to the rest of the world within thirty years.

Initially, this barrage of expectations frustrated me. However, in her typical unflappable nature, Janai didn't let it bother her the slightest bit. She's always had that "we've got this" mentality. But for me, the notion that I would be responsible for my child's success seemed a little unfair. Sure, I'm his dad and I do have a duty to steer him in the right direction, but I didn't give him a personality—God did. I didn't give him a brain—God did. What if Tony simply hated school and was a mean-hearted individual? Did we as his parents have any control over that? Or what if he wasn't the sharpest tool in the shed? Why should we be held accountable for things that ultimately would be out of our control? That was my issue with these expectations. Just because the parents did well doesn't mean the children will…right?

Time has answered that question for me. Even though I've only been at this parenting thing for five years, I already understand why these expectations have been stamped upon us. The truth is, Tony, Jace, and Mavyn are privileged in specific ways that only come from having parents who have achieved a certain societal stature. At the age of five, Tony begs to come practice medicine and take care of critically ill patients with Daddy. At the age of three, Jace has his own stethoscope and can pronounce the word. As an infant, while playing with her dolls, Mavyn can already envision a real-life Doc McStuffins in her mother. Their reality is one that many other children will never have, and might only see on television. They have a very real and tangible head start in life. It is a true competitive advantage.

In the premedical community, I have developed the reputation of "mentor" to many students. They know they can turn to my team and our resources for guidance. From physician shadowing opportunities, to recruitment information, to choosing the right medical school, we get it all. These messages come from young dreamers all over the country who not only aspire to become medical doctors, but are also capable of doing so. However, a good amount of them will never make it. In many circumstances, the number one roadblock to bringing this dream to fruition is poor access to mentors and sponsors within the medical community. I do my best to support them; however, like any other human being, I have limited time. The unfortunate thing about such situations is that more often than is acceptable, these students don't have access to other medical mentors. And when they do get access, it's often too late in the game to have a significant impact on their course. These kids simply lack the necessary exposure to make their dreams reality. Let me ask you this: How in the world will they compete with my children who have had this exposure from day one?

Reluctantly, I recognize this advantage. I say reluctantly because everyone wants to be the underdog. If you're expected to win but don't, that's a little embarrassing. It always sounds better to build your way to success from a disadvantaged perspective. However, it would be foolish of me not to acknowledge the advantage which my children have, and even more foolish not to capitalize on it. As a matter of fact, not doing so would be the equivalent of parental malpractice. No matter how bad I'd like to pretend that my children are starting off on the same playing field as everyone else, it's simply not the case. As it stands today, they are privileged.

Now, here's the kicker. Those born with "fewer" resources in life aren't necessarily at a disadvantage. Or at least they don't have to be. On the contrary, if they possess what the famous fashion mogul Daymond John calls "the Power of Broke," they have quite the upper hand. Having less in material resources does not mean that an individual has less in mental resources. Equal mental capacity with fewer resources can ignite unparalleled creativity, which puts people in unique positions of opportunity that can propel them to various levels of success.

Think about it. There are tons of wealthy people who started out with close to nothing. Ask Daymond John, and he'll probably tell you that had he not been broke, he never would have become the world-renowned businessman we know him to be today. So, here's the truth you need to know: All children have an advantage in some shape or form; the determining factor in whether or not that advantage will be cultivated is the parent (or guardian). In this book, I will show you how some parents have done just that to help their children become doctors and leaders in society.

My Why

I wrote this book because of a young mother who reached out to me. She had watched one of my *Black Men in White Coats* videos and took it upon herself to contact me for the sake of her child. "Dr. Dale," she wrote, "I am a young mother raising a son. I want him to do well in life and could really use your help. Please, what can I do to help my son become a doctor?" Her passion and desire to give her son that advantage in life were palpable. Clearly, she was willing to give everything she had to see him become what she viewed as successful. The fact that she took the time to contact me, a complete stranger, demonstrated this truth. It also suggested that she had limited access to people who do what I do in society.

This mother changed my perspective on the strategies my team and I were implementing to provide opportunities for young dreamers with aspirations of donning the white coat. I also get contacted by parents who have direct access to a multitude of resources. It might even surprise you to know that other doctors ask me for advice on these same issues. The reason this young mother's message was so attractive to me was because at the time, I couldn't recall another instance when a parent who was not a healthcare professional had gone out of the way to contact me for the sake of his or her child. Sure, the ones who see me at various events ask questions in person, but she was the first to reach out in this fashion. Since then, however, it has now happened several times, and I have come to appreciate that many parents are looking for the information in this book.

This mother changed my perspective on the efforts my team and I were investing to provide opportunities for young dreamers who have aspirations of donning the white coat. Up until then, I had been completely focused on mentoring students. I founded DiverseMedicine Inc., Black Men in White Coats, and PreMed STAR—all with the intent of providing the necessary resources and inspiration for our students' success. While a great many of them have benefitted from our organizations, there's always a large cohort that we can't reach. These students are active, and from an outside perspective, appear to be doing all the right things. However, it often becomes apparent that many lack certain life disciplines and experiences that are required for success. While it's true that these keys to success can be acquired at an older age, students who possess them earlier in life have an advantage. Those students who learn early on how to be successful likely had parents, teachers, and mentors educating them in these arenas. They certainly didn't learn those lessons on their own.

The Diversity Example

Volumes of research have demonstrated the importance of diversity, and we know it improves outcomes in various fields. For decades, healthcare professionals—and others with vested interests—have sought to increase diversity in the medical workforce. Millions, if not billions, of dollars have been poured into this endeavor in the form of scholarships, summer programs, fee assistance opportunities, and the list goes on and on and on. Leaders across the country, my team included, have dedicated themselves to this mission. With each new medical student, my team members and I get ecstatic about the perceived progress. But the numbers show that diversity in the medical workforce, as it pertains to underrep-

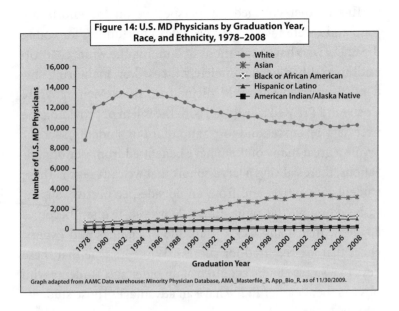

Figure 14: U.S. MD Physicians by Graduation Year, Race, and Ethnicity, 1978–2008

Graph adapted from AAMC Data warehouse: Minority Physician Database, AMA_Masterfile_R, App_Bio_R, as of 11/30/2009.

resented minorities, has been relatively stagnant. According to data from the Association of American Medical Colleges (AAMC), the number of Hispanic and Black physicians has not significantly increased over an approximate thirty-year time span.

Bearing this in mind, one would have to ask, "How is it possible that all of the money we've poured into diversifying the medical workforce hasn't made a dent?" I believe one of two things is occurring. First, it could be that these diversity numbers would be much worse without this cash influx and nonmonetary resources. Perhaps there would have been an alarming downtrend in the number of minority physicians. The second possibility, and in my opinion the more likely and more important contributor, is that our strategies, while valiant, have been suboptimal.

Consider this extreme example. You're starting a circus, and the feature act will be an elephant performance. You purchase the elephant and hire a trainer. To prepare the elephant for his tricks, you put him in all sorts of programs and throw all sorts of resources at him. When the big day comes for him to perform live at your long-anticipated circus, he's just not ready. The show begins, and he sits there motionless. When prompted to proceed with his various stunts, he stumbles around the rink.

What was the problem? It's quite simple. Yes, you gave the elephant abundant resources, but you never taught and empowered his trainer. Keep in mind, this trainer was the individual most invested and most responsible for the elephant's success. However, you didn't provide the knowledge and tools needed for him to do his job in preparing the elephant. Again, this is an extreme and ridiculous example, but the fact remains, it's more important to properly empower the teacher than the student. Empowered teachers can begin imparting the disciplines of success in their students early on. Oh, I should also mention that you are the teacher!

A New Challenge

Recognizing this truth, I was left with a new challenge. For the most part, high school students and those younger aren't confident about their future career decisions and rarely go out of their way to investigate the various options. More important is that they don't know the disciplines of success, and in many instances, are altogether oblivious to the concept. Most of my time and energy are dedicated towards students. Barely any of my resources are reserved for parents, the people most invested in the lives of the very children we seek to help. What makes us think we can help these students accomplish their goals better than their own parents can? With this mother's cry for help, my new challenge became, how can I empower parents to raise doctors?

I am uncertain why it has taken me this long to appreciate this obstacle and engage it. It should have been evident to me all along. As an adolescent, my friends' parents would ask, "Dale, can you talk to so and so…help him get on the right track?" Nothing has changed in all those years. It's a different generation of parents, but they're still asking, "Dr. Dale, can you talk to my son? Dr. Dale, can you talk to my daughter?"

It's taken some time, but I now understand that instead of focusing solely on the student, we should have been providing the resources to the parents as well. Students usually aren't thinking about what their lives will look like in ten, twenty, or thirty years. Parents, on the other hand, are constantly worrying about the future of their babies. This young mother made something very clear to me: Parents want to know how to provide their children with every possible advantage! They just need other parents who have done it to tell them how.

That's where this book comes into play. My intention is to give you an advantage!

Napoleon Hill's Strategy

When I told my mother I was going to write a book called *How to Raise a Doctor,* she laughed at me. "Dale, when was the last time you raised a doctor? Your oldest child is only five." Her point was well taken. Although I, with exceptional guidance, and only by the grace of God, had successfully navigated the journey to becoming a practicing physician, I still was not fully credentialed to tell other parents how to raise a doctor. Why would they listen to me? I hadn't done it. That being the case, I pondered letting it go. Perhaps someone else, a more qualified individual, would step up and write this much-needed book.

But for some reason, I couldn't shake the idea. It seemed to follow me everywhere I went. The more people learned about the various organizations I had founded, the more that infamous question would come back to me: "Dr. Dale, what do I need to do to help my child become a doctor?" Inadvertently, I had put myself in another position of expectation that called me to action in accordance with a biblical verse I live by, "To whom much is given, much shall be required" (Luke 12:48). I knew I had been given much; therefore, I knew I had to write this book. But like my mom asked, how could I do this if I've never raised a doctor? There had to be a way to answer the calling of so many parents.

I thought back to my very first day of Internal Medicine residency at Duke. As a young doctor, still wet behind the ears, I heard something that has stuck with me ever since. During our orientation session, Dr. Diana B. McNeil, who was our program director at the time, bestowed these wise words upon my cohort; "When you leave this program, you might not always know the answer to the problem, but you'll always know how to find it." The truth of the matter is, nobody really cares where the information comes from, as long as the information is right. I haven't raised a doctor myself, but I know an awful lot of people who have. Furthermore, adding my personal expertise in mentoring and student development to the wisdom of these parents truly completes the picture. This book can help you set your children on a path to success.

Napoleon Hill is one of history's best-selling and most influential writers. He is the author of *Think and Grow Rich*. In this book, Hill outlines several concepts that helped make the affluent of his day wealthy. Ultimately, these same concepts would make Hill wealthy as well. When he began working on this book, Hill wasn't the well-to-do author and speaker who most people came to know him as. As a matter of fact, he was a broke journalist. But when Andrew Carnegie, who at that time was one of the world's richest people, summoned him, Hill's life would change forever. According to Hill, Carnegie tasked him with the job of interviewing the wealthiest and most successful people of their day. His assignment was to detail the mindset and actions which led to their extraordinary accomplishments. Hill did as tasked, and in doing so, ended up with a book that has sold over twenty million copies and influenced some of today's greatest minds.

My approach to writing this book is similar to Hill's. The key difference however, is I actually know what it's like to be a medical doctor, whereas Hill didn't know what it was like to be rich (until he became immensely successful following the completion of his assignment from Carnegie). Over the years, I have connected with many highly intelligent and successful individuals. Together, we have journeyed the road of medicine, and I have watched them develop into some of America's top clinicians. Many have shared childhood stories highlighting the importance of their parents in achieving their goals. They haven't raised doctors, but their parents have. I haven't raised a doctor, but my parents have. In order to deliver our parents' secrets to you, I have interviewed them, and compiled their top principles deemed essential in raising a doctor.

I should also mention one thing. I've titled this book *How to Raise a Doctor* because it takes a certain type of person to become a doctor. However, the heart of the title is *how to raise a leader*. The principles taught in this book are not specific for medicine. If you can raise a doctor, you can raise a leader in just about any other profession. Success is success, and the same principles can get you there in any arena of life. My goal in writing this book is for parents to develop a clear understanding of the intentionality and structure necessary to mold your child into someone who will positively impact the world. As my friend Tammy Kling says, "We're looking to make world changers!"

Now back to the question at hand: "Dr. Dale, what do I need to do to help my child become a doctor?" This is a loaded question with tremendous implications. Consider the perspective of individuals coming from a disadvantaged background. Often, their resources are limited, including their academic network. I might not have raised a doctor, but this one thing is crystal clear to me: If you don't have people around you who have achieved the goal you dream of, more than likely you won't get there. As former surgeon general, Dr. Jocelyn Elders, often says, "You can't be what you can't see."

What do I need to do to help my child become a doctor?

When I hear that question, I'm not just hearing a single mother or hardworking father seeking to someday say, "My baby's a doc!" I know what they're really asking: "Dr. Dale, what can I do to change generations of misfortune and transform the legacy of my descendants into one of contentment and prosperity?" That's the true question in their heart! And those individuals who come from wealth are asking a very similar question: "Dr. Dale, what can I do to maintain generations of wealth, prosperity, and a respected societal stature for my family?" At the end of the day, it's about familial legacy.

My answer to both their questions would be to raise a doctor. Above all other fields, medicine is the one that provides the highest likelihood of having a high-income career, which can establish and maintain generational wealth (assuming the student is disciplined enough and has the appropriate resources). It transforms lives, literally taking some people from poverty to financial abundance. And unlike basketball, hip-hop, or film, it is within reach for the average person. Ultimately, providing a true understanding of the basic principles necessary to raise a doctor can have a significant socioeconomic impact within a community.

Only in Medicine

The famous entertainment promoter Don King has a well-known saying that goes, "Only in America!" I have my own saying: "Only in medicine!" Only in medicine can you develop a certain stature of respect given to you by the vast majority of the population. When I walk in a hospital without my white coat, nobody gives me a second look. Half the time, my own colleagues don't recognize or acknowledge me. But when that coat is on my back, people stand and salute. Not because I am anybody special, but because I am a doctor. Our work is thought to be special, and people respect that. They understand what the white coat symbolizes and what we, as doctors, have gone through to obtain it. Suddenly, I get smiles and handshakes, and people address me as "sir" (even those decades older than me).

Only in medicine will a perfect stranger trust you with their deepest and darkest secrets. Husbands and wives will tell me things that they would never consider mentioning to their spouse. I am obliged to mention that I don't endorse this as I believe husbands and wives should have no secrets. But this is the reality about the trust people put in physicians. They feel that they can share these secrets with me just because I'm a doctor. Only in medicine can you essentially guarantee yourself a stable salary in the top 3 percent of Americans. Once you get your foot in the door, your course is nearly set. That's my motto, "Only in medicine!"

As we embark on this journey together, I'd like to make it clear that this book is for me just as much as it is for you. As I write this now, I have yet to conduct my first interview with any of the parents of my fellow physicians. In other words, I will be learning right alongside you. Consider this a real-life experiment. In writing this book, I am forcing the issue and making myself accountable to do the research necessary for my own children's success. I can't see the future and have absolutely no idea what their professions will be. I can't even promise that they will be societal leaders. But I can promise that I will do everything in my power to bring that to fruition. This book is part of my attempt to make it happen, and I am sharing it with you so you can do the same for your children. In the end, when your children succeed, mine do as well. Let's do this together!

PARENT PERSPECTIVE

Help your Child Find What They Love

Encouraging your child to pursue what they love is a process, one that takes on a different character as time passes and your child matures. *Trust that what you love is worthwhile. And pursue with vigor the things that are important to you, regardless of what others may think.* This was a guiding principle in our home.

Early on, we laid the foundation of absolute truths. Family and faith were always first. Our children experienced unconditional love, and they learned the importance of duty, loyalty, respect and a "we" family identity. A sense of safety, security, and self-confidence was firmly established and enforced within the home. Our hope was that this early foundation would largely shape what the children later found important to them, and what they would come to love.

In the middle years of their upbringing, the children learned the difference between things that bring us pleasure, things that are important, and those very few things we actually love. Life's normal experiences, including conflict resolutions within the family, were the stage on which it all played out. They learned that whatever was important to them was also important to their parents. The parental role shifted from teacher of truths to guider of the process by which the children discovered for themselves the hand they had been dealt in life and how they would play it.

The later formative years are a time to translate values and life experiences into significant life choices. When John graduated from Notre Dame he was uncertain how he wanted to go about making a difference in the lives of others. As his classmates were moving on to attractive careers or prestigious graduate programs, John took a step back. As his parents, we appreciated his thoughtfulness and patience to make the right decision. He spent two years working to make ends meet and volunteered at local medical clinics and hospitals. From those experiences, his own path emerged. It was on to medical school and a concurrent life of public service. John found what he genuinely loves! Mission accomplished. Happy child. Proud parents. Prayers of thanks to God.

ANNE AND ROBERT CORKER
Parents of Dr. John Corker

2

DON'T RAISE A DOCTOR

A leader is one who knows the way,
goes the way, and shows the way.

—John Maxwell

I know what you're thinking, I thought this book was about *how to raise a doctor, and now this guy is telling me not to raise a doctor!* That's exactly right. I'm telling you to not raise a doctor. Instead, raise a leader, and let that leader become a doctor, lawyer, author, president, or whatever he or she dreams to be. Let that leader change the world for the better! Hone in on your child's gifts and nurture them to full development. This is what all parents should want for their children.

Would you believe me if I told you most parents I spoke with didn't set out to raise a doctor? Well, it's true. Only 22 percent of the doctors' parents surveyed reported that they intentionally raised their child to become a doctor. This means that the clear majority, 78 percent, did not.

At this juncture, your question is (or should be): Should I intentionally raise my child to become a medical doctor? The fact that you're reading this book would suggest you might be leaning that way already. I can help you answer the question right now with one finding from my survey. Among the 22 percent of parents who intentionally raised their children to become doctors, 71 percent of the children wanted to be doctors throughout their childhood. So, to answer your question, you should intentionally raise your child to become a doctor if he or she wants to be a doctor.

The Power of Suggestion

Seventy-one percent of the children who were intentionally raised to become doctors wanted to be doctors since childhood. With this finding in mind, the question then arises: Was it the influence of the parents that led these children to dream of careers in medicine, or did the desire truly belong to the child?

It's true that parents can influence their children to pursue medicine. Mine did. The power of suggestion is a real phenomenon that can change behaviors, beliefs, and desires. To show you just how real it is, I'll share the work of Dr. Julia Shaw. Dr. Shaw is a psychologist who has done extensive work in the field of memory and suggestion. Her research has shown the world how easy it is to influence the beliefs of other people. In a ground-breaking study, Dr. Shaw interviewed parents of college students to learn about their children's upbringing. Next, she identified sixty of these students who had never committed a crime, then held a series of three interviews with each of them. The students were under the impression that the study was simply about their childhood memories. The true objective, however, was to see whether or not they could be influenced to believe lies about their past.

During interview one, Dr. Shaw initially discussed true events that had happened to the student. Once they felt comfortable, she introduced a lie pertaining to a crime the student had committed. Initially, students tended to deny the crime, but Shaw used social manipulation techniques such as a childhood friend's name to make the situation seem real. By the third interview a few weeks later, 70 percent of the students had admitted they committed a crime that never happened. Amazing!

If Dr. Shaw could use the power of suggestion to convince 70 percent of her research subjects that they committed a crime that never even happened, then of course a parent can use this same power of suggestion to influence a child to pursue a career in medicine. The real question is whether or not it matters. Is it a bad thing to influence your children to chase dreams that you believe are magnificent? I don't think so at all. The desire to achieve anything in life has to come from somewhere.

My daughter is an infant and is unable to plant her own tree. If I take her out to our backyard and plant a seed for her, then let her water and nurture it as she grows older, who does that tree belong to? I'd say it's hers. By the same token, dreams planted by parents, but developed by children, belong to the children. This is the most important aspect to grasp in this book: *the dream must belong to the child.*

So, should you use the power of suggestion as a parenting tactic? Absolutely! Doing so would be responsible of you. Expose your children to good things and suggest they consider learning more about them. Remember, I said that you should intentionally raise your child to become a doctor only if he or she wants to become a doctor. The challenge then arises in knowing if your child wants to pursue that path. The only way to find out is for someone to suggest it along the way. What better someone than you?

Immigrants Raise Doctors

Another fascinating finding in my survey was that 64 percent of the parents who intentionally raised their children to become doctors were immigrants to the United States. This becomes even more interesting when you consider the estimates that up to 27 percent of US physicians are foreign born. And keep in mind, that number isn't including their first-generation children who ultimately become doctors. Although I wasn't expecting this finding, I wasn't surprised by it. Why? Because it's my story.

> *Education has been the single most important thing for my family, and it's literally changed everything.*
> —ELISA VILLANUEVA BEARD, CEO OF TEACH FOR AMERICA

MaDear came to the United States at age seventeen and Papa at age nineteen. Like most immigrants, they came in search of opportunity, and education was their ticket to find it. Papa had, and still has, an unparalleled work ethic. Unlike most college students, he didn't have the luxury of completing college in four years. He did it all in two and a half. Training a child is expensive, and the price tag can be even higher when doing so in a foreign country. My grandparents couldn't afford for Papa to stay in the States without him having a real income, so he did what he had to in order to earn the degree he came for. That meant taking up to twenty-seven credits hours in one semester while working full time. Life wasn't easy.

As a child, not once did I hear my parents complain about

how difficult things were for them. They did what was necessary to get our family to the next level. Even after earning her MBA (master in business administration), my mother worked as a store clerk just to make ends meet until we could get on our feet. Challenge after challenge and sacrifice after sacrifice, Papa and MaDear remained appreciative of their opportunities.

"One of the most important things we did in raising you all was sacrifice."

These were Papa's words when I asked him to list the ten most important things they did in raising doctors.

He continued, "There were career opportunities that your mother and I could have taken, but we knew it wouldn't be the best thing for your upbringing. Had we done those things, we wouldn't have been able to do the things that were necessary for you all to be where you are today."

Papa actually wanted to become a medical doctor, but didn't have the same type of guidance he'd later be able to provide to his own children. He earned his Ph.D. but was unable to go back to medical school as planned because there were hungry mouths to feed at home.

"Had I gone to medical school, it would have been too difficult for us to raise you all up the way we wanted. As young immigrants, we didn't have a strong infrastructure to support our family. It took some time for us to develop that."

But their sacrifices paid off. Papa and MaDear raised four professionals. Growing up, they always told us that their measure of success would be whether or not their children could surpass their accomplishments. Everything they did was intentionally setting us up to do just that. They used the power of suggestion to introduce careers that they believed would bring us joy and a sense of purpose. In their opinion, medicine was the epitome of that. Furthermore, they constantly reinforced that as doctors, we could find jobs anywhere in the world. In their minds, this was truly the best career possible.

A Scary Profession

There's a particular profession that has horrendous statistics. Individuals in this field are over twice as likely to commit suicide than the general public. During their first year on the job, depression rates are as high as 30 percent, and suicidal ideation has been reported as high as 25 percent. Prescription drug abuse is problematic, and the divorce rate is 20 percent greater than the public. It's a scary profession!

If you haven't figured it out yet, I'm talking about the medical profession.

Most doctors find it amusing when their friends in other fields complain about long fourteen-to-sixteen-hour workdays. Or when they wax poetic about how difficult and stressful their job is. I've even had people make a direct comparison between their job and that of doctors in attempt to demonstrate they've got it tougher than we do. In my honest opinion, there are very few professions, the military being one of them, that put people through greater stress and turmoil than medicine. Of course, there are outliers in every field, but by and large, medicine takes the cake.

During your medical training, you're constantly being beaten down—mentally, physically, and spiritually—as if someone put you in the boxing ring with Mike Tyson, then tied your feet together so you can't get away. Day in and day out, you have to stand there and take a whooping. It's not an easy journey, and you should be fully aware of what medicine entails prior to encouraging your children to pursue it. Very few, if any at all, get through this training unscathed. As an example, let me share one of the worst periods of my life with you, one during which that triple beatdown almost gave me a TKO.

Towards the end of my residency, my son became ill with a viral gastroenteritis. During that same time, a patient—I'll call her Jane—was admitted to the hospital, and I was the senior resident physician caring for her. She had pneumonia, and we treated her with the appropriate medications. On her third day, because she had been doing so well and none of her microbiology studies had returned with any bacteria requiring IV antibiotics, we made a plan to discharge her with oral antibiotics, and treat her for less dangerous infections (this is the standard of care according to practice guidelines).

That day, my son's gastroenteritis hit me big time! I began vomiting at work and was instructed to go home. Nobody wanted me to get them sick, so I was quickly rushed out of the hospital and had to ask a colleague to discharge Jane for me. That was a Sunday, and I ended up having to take the next day off as well. If memory serves me correct, that was the only sick day I had as a resident physician. For the most part, doctors only miss work when they are vomiting or near incapacitated. Denzel Washington said it best in his movie *John Q*, "People get sick on Saturday, don't they?" What's implied here is that doctors can't get the same time off that everyone else gets. Healthcare must be available around the clock.

When I came back to work, I saw that Jane was readmitted to the hospital, but this time to the intensive care unit. She had gone into fulminant respiratory failure and was placed on life support. Nobody saw this coming. Jane subsequently died, and her microbiology studies returned with a very dangerous bacteria known as community-acquired methicillin resistant *Staphylococcus Aureus* (CA-MRSA). My assumption is that she initially had a viral pneumonia then developed a superinfection with this nasty bacteria. I remember her sister coming by the bedside confused and upset. I prayed with her and apologized that I couldn't have done more. I felt at fault, and the what-ifs began running through my head: What if we had kept her in the hospital one more day? What if we hadn't changed her antibiotics? What if we called to check on her the day after discharge? Although our treatment strategy was appropriate, it was still very hard to deal with.

That was the second lowest moment of my life (the first being when one of my best friends died during my teenage years). If ever I came close to depression, that would have been the time. I was physically beat from eighty-hour work weeks and a viral gastroenteritis. I was mentally beat from caring for so many patients. I was spiritually beat because I wasn't sure why God had allowed this young woman to die. What many people don't fully grasp when considering the lives of doctors is that we really do deal with high-stakes life-and-death situations (especially in my field of critical care medicine). Seeing so many people die can take a toll on you, and really mess with your mind. This is the reality of being a physician.

So, you want your child to become a medical doctor? If that's the case, try saying this out loud: "My goal for my child is to become a professional who is at increased risk of suicide, prescription drug abuse, divorce, depression, and works an absurd number of hours, many times going days with little or no sleep. That's what I want for my child!"

Really…is it? I'll be honest with you, there is no way I'm raising any of my children with that end goal. Do I love the field of medicine? Of course, I do! Would I do it all over again? Emphatically yes! But my goal is to raise leaders, and if they choose to pursue medicine, I will give them all the resources they need to make it happen. However, by no means will I force this upon them. It has to be their choice.

It's also possible that children who wanted to be doctors

since childhood weren't influenced by their parents to chase this dream. Perhaps their parents didn't plant the seed, but simply identified this desire in their children then focused their efforts to make those dreams a reality. Even though they raised their children to become doctors, they did not force the career upon them. The desire belonged to the child outside of the parents' will.

What I hope you gather from this chapter is that if your child reaches a point when he or she reliably expresses to you that medicine is not the right field, you should not push them against their will. Not only will you build a relationship of resentment, but you might increase their risk pertaining to various negative life outcomes.

Recently, I was invited to speak at UCLA. While there, I had the chance to meet with many leaders of their academic medical center, including Associate Dean Lynn Gordon. Dr. Gordon is a well-accomplished neuro-ophthalmologist, and her husband is the chairman of pathology at the medical school there. Together, they have three children; one of whom is completing his medical school training at the time of my writing.

I took the opportunity during our encounter to ask her what the most important thing was pertaining to raising a doctor. Her response was as follows: "The most important thing we did was pay attention to what our children loved and what they wanted to do. Then we loved them with all our hearts and helped them do it. We never wanted any of them to feel pressured to practice medicine."

Reflecting on her statement, I am able to see how my parents did just that. Although they would have loved for all of their children to pursue careers in medicine, they never forced it upon us. My oldest brother, Anthony, works in the field of information technology, and my sister, Anthonette, is a lawyer. Their respected careers fit them perfectly. Curious to know how my parents shepherded all of us into the right fields, I asked MaDear what the secret was.

"All of you were given the same opportunities," she told me. "The same way we suggested medicine to you and Daniel is the way we did for your older siblings. When we provided it to the two of you as an option, you were interested, so we continued to encourage it. Your older siblings weren't nearly as interested. You have to know your children. It didn't fit their personalities, so we continued to suggest other things. The most important thing, however, is that we instilled values of excellence and hard work in you all. That is the key, no matter what field your child wants to go into."

I'd be willing to bet a nickel that every parent I interviewed would agree with my mom's statement. The values you instill in your children are more important than the profession you desire for them. Most of the parents in the survey did not intentionally raise their kids to become doctors, but all of them raised their children with certain values of leadership. Setting out to raise a doctor is myopic. Setting out to raise a real leader is heroic. You don't want to raise a doctor, you want to raise a leader! Your child becoming a doctor is just a nice by-product of him or her developing into a leader—with your guidance.

One of my mentors, Mr. Joel Wiggins, once told me that it was my responsibility as a parent to know what my children should become and make it happen. At the time, my oldest son must have been about three years old, and I couldn't fathom such a responsibility. Initially, I understood Joel to be saying that I must choose a career for my kids and use my resources to get them there. Over the years, as I've spent more time with him, I've paid keen attention to the way he speaks of his own children. He often identifies their strong points and is just as good at noting their weak areas. Typically, not in the same conversations, he puts forth likely careers for his daughters (his son is all grown up and out of the house now). Joel and his wife, Katrina, are very good at providing a variety of options for their daughters, then encouraging them to focus in key areas.

It has taken some years of watching their family for me to properly understand what he meant, but now I get it. Every child is gifted in certain areas and has interest in certain areas. As parents, it is our responsibility to study our children closely in order to identify and align their gifts and interests. Once this alignment occurs, teach your child how to exploit it not only for financial gain, but more importantly, for a positive societal impact.

The constant theme among the parents I interviewed is that at some point, they figured out what their children should become, then they did what they could to bring it to fruition. They did not force them to become doctors, but rather suggested the option and ushered them to success.

PARENT PERSPECTIVE

Faith & Perseverance

Raising my son, Kenneth, was a privilege given to me by God and as such, I recognized that success was not tied to the specific career he chose, but in learning to love God above all else. My goal was to teach him to seek God first while relying upon His promises. As a result, I believe God granted him the privilege of achieving a position of leadership as an orthopedic surgeon.

The most important advice I gave my son was to persevere through trials, reminding him that when he follows God's will, God is faithful to provide the strength needed, *"for you have need of endurance so that when you have done the will of God you may receive what is promised"* (Hebrews 10:36). Kenneth had many trials, even as a child. He wasn't the most popular, he was labeled at-risk in elementary, and his intelligence often worked against him. Even within the family, because I demanded that he be both helpful and respectful, Kenneth was often taken advantage of while others didn't have these demands. I wanted to build his character and work ethic. As he grew older, it was my desire that he would learn to press on while counting on the mercies of God, and he did.

It was also important for Kenneth to have the right perspective of wealth. I wanted him to understand that God's provisions were not given exclusively to fulfill his personal desires, but to build God's kingdom through those with whom he has the privilege to influence. As he has progressed in his career, I've been extremely proud to see him put this understanding to practice. In keeping the faith, he has persevered in doing good, and by the grace of God, Kenneth is impacting lives both in, and out of the operating room.

LILENE CALDWELL
Mother of Dr. Kenneth Caldwell

3

MY BABY'S A DOCTOR

You don't have to be famous. You just have to make your
mother and father proud of you.

—MERYL STREEP

Say out loud, "My baby's a doctor!"

Are you all alone? If so, stand up and scream out at the top
of your lungs, "My baby's a doctor!" Feels good, doesn't it?

I just did it, and it felt great!

I'm guessing you want your child to be a doctor or some
sort of societal leader. After all, you're reading this book. Don't
be shy about it; it's okay to confess your dream. It's also okay
to proclaim it. You're not alone. If this is something that you
really want for your child, how can you expect it to happen if
you can't be honest with yourself?

Year after year, parents rank medicine as one of the top
fields they'd like their children to pursue. Polls have demonstrated that over nine in ten parents would encourage their
child to work towards a medical career. That's 90 percent! Let

me say it again—you're not alone! As a matter of fact, not encouraging your child to be a medical doctor would put you in the minority. This parental desire has become the norm. So, feel free to scream it out loud once more, but this time even louder: "My baby's a doctor!"

A Medical Love Affair

Society has a secret love affair with medical doctors. It's actually a love-hate relationship—and an obsessive one at that. Just consider television programming over the past several decades. Let's play a little game. Take one minute and name as many doctor shows as you can. Go!

Several immediately came to mind for me. Let's take it way back in the day. Starring as Marcus Welby, MD, award-winning actor Robert Young made you trust us. Marcus Welby was America's doctor. He was a veteran of the US Navy and a widower. Just stop and think about that. Military veteran, widower, medical doctor—how can you not love this guy? His back story alone won the hearts of men and women. Dr. Welby was portrayed as a loving physician who would do anything he could for his patients. Furthermore, he was an excellent teacher and colleague. He was the doctor parents wanted their kids to be.

Fast-forward a few decades, and we've got the medical drama *ER*. For fifteen years, the series showed viewers just how exciting a doctor's job can be. It made you revere us. Knowing that when the world is falling apart and people are dying, there are doctors who remain cool, calm, and collected. You developed faith in our capabilities under stress. *ER* showed you the inside action of the hospital, making us out to be superheroes. As an ICU physician, I can relate to this show. When things get wild and crazy, family members get out of the way and place their trust in us.

Here's something fascinating I learned from *ER*: Doctors can be more than doctors. This wasn't highlighted on the show itself, but rather in its creator. Michael Crichton obtained his medical degree from Harvard Medical School. *ER* was the product of his own experiences during his residency training. He first proposed this screenplay in the 1970s without success. Just under twenty years later, he wrote the now classic novel *Jurassic Park*, which subsequently opened doors for other opportunities, including *ER*. Remember to teach your children that their jobs don't define them. The mere fact that you are reading this book is evidence that doctors can do more than care for patients.

Scrubs! Who could ever forget about this classic comedy? It made viewers think doctors have a sense of humor and are fun to be around. For the most part, I'd say this is true. Many of my colleagues will tell you that this sitcom, above all others, most closely reflected the life we lived during our medical training. Medical residency is tough, and to survive it, you must have a sense of humor. The stress is way too high not to pull a few pranks and crack a couple of jokes from time to time. Scrubs showed its audience that even doctors "got jokes."

House M.D. was one of my favorites. During medical school, several classmates would gather at my house on Tuesday nights to watch the latest episodes. It portrays doctors as not just cool—we're really cool. Even though this genius "Mr. Solve It All" physician was quite the jerk on the show, you had to love his swag. House isn't your good old Marcus Welby. He's a rude smart aleck who rides a motorcycle. For some odd reason, that seems to be what society wants today. And if society wants it, Hollywood supplies it. They showed viewers that doctors can be that way too. On the flip side of the coin, House also has an addiction to prescription pain medications.

This unfortunate and undesirable trait showed viewers that doctors are human, and we face the same struggles as the rest of society.

Grey's Anatomy showed viewers that we're sexy. There isn't a single ugly doctor on that show. So not only are we caring, smart, funny, and cool, but we're also gorgeous. And of course, you know what happens when you put a bunch of gorgeous people together in one environment…fireworks! Okay, just so you know, medical training isn't really like that. At least it wasn't for me. Perhaps I was the odd ball out, and everyone else was living the glamorous life of Meredith Grey.

We've hit on some of the fictional characters, but let's not forget about the award-winning talk show *The Doctors* and those real-life doctors on television: Dr. Mehmet Oz, Dr. Sanjay Gupta, and Dr. Drew. All of these have become household names. There have even been reality shows focused on the lifestyle of doctors. So, do you see it yet? Are you able to understand how the media is partially responsible for America's obsession with medicine?

Don't get me wrong, I think this is a good thing. I absolutely love my life as a physician, and it's true that there are similarities between what you see on TV and how we live. I'm simply pointing out that society is enamored with our profession. Surely this contributes to the desire of those nine in ten parents who would encourage their children to pursue medicine.

Okay, say it again. "My baby's a doctor!"

Now let me ask you this: What feeling do you get when you say that phrase?

Pride, isn't it? Even though it hasn't happened yet, it still puts a smile on your face the same way it did my mother's.

I remember the look in her eyes when my older brother Daniel became a medical doctor. We threw a big party for him at a local hotel, and my folks were on cloud nine. I'm not sure I'd ever seen them happier. It was almost as if they were the ones getting the degree that day, and in a sense, they were. His accomplishments were their accomplishments. Throughout his premedical days and even while in medical school, my parents had been extremely supportive of him the same way they'd be of me a couple years later. And on that day when my brother got his diploma, they were finally able to say those words, "My baby's a doctor."

There are few prouder moments in a mother's life than when her child graduates. What's funny is that the graduation can be at any level. When my son graduated kindergarten, my wife was ecstatic. Family members were invited from out of state, outfits were specially chosen, and the cameras were prepped. The way my mama bear (my wife) was acting, you'd have thought my boy earned a doctorate. When I saw how happy Janai was when Tony grabbed his kindergarten diploma, I couldn't help but envision how happy she'll be if he chooses to pursue and one day earn a medical degree. For all intents and purposes, the doctorate is the pinnacle of institutional education. There is no higher degree to be achieved.

Okay, your kid gets a few extra letters after their name. MD, DO, Ph.D....whatever! They're smart; you know it, I know it, and the world knows it. So what? What's all this doctor fuss about anyway? They're other excellent careers out there, and medicine isn't the only respected field. What's so special about doctors that makes it okay for nine out of ten parents to encourage this profession for their children? The answer to this question is simple. Societal stature. Even more important than money, the medical degree lends instant stature and credibility, no matter the context. This is the real reason parents want their children to become physicians.

Although media highly influences the perceptions of doctors, unlike in the entertainment industry, the desire to pursue medicine as a profession begins in your own backyard. Not everyone knows an entertainer, but at some point, just about everyone interacts with a physician. Okay, you might know a superstar athlete on the high school or collegiate level, but that's a completely different lifestyle than the pros. The only reason most people have any sort of understanding of how professional athletes live is because they watch them on TV. That's not the case for medicine. You know how we live because you see us on regular basis, and many of us live in, or come from, communities you can relate to. So, when you say that you want to raise a doctor, it's in part because you have had personal experiences with doctors you respect, and you would like your child to follow that model. It's all about stature, and physicians carry a lot of it within communities.

When my wife and I meet new people, we do our best not to share our profession early in the conversation. This might sound strange, but letting people know you're a doctor at first encounter can be somewhat embarrassing. What's even worse is letting them know your spouse is one too. As soon as we divulge that bit of information, the focus of the conversation typically shifts to us. The only time this doesn't happen is when we are among well-to-do businessmen and women. They couldn't care less what we do for a living. Otherwise, the story is typically the same.

"You're a doctor? You must be smart! What kind of doctor are you? Where do you practice? Are you taking any new patients? My dad needs a lung doctor..."

Soon after, many people begin to downplay their own professions.

"Oh, I'm just a [insert career here]. Nothing like what you do."

I can't tell you how many times I've had this conversation.

It gets so bad that my wife started to tell people where she works and attempts to avoid sharing what she does there. By no means are we ashamed of it. As I said before, it just becomes embarrassing when people immediately place you on a pedestal.

Respect is among life's most desired attributes. Parents want their children to be respected, so of course they'd want their kids to be a part of history's most respected profession. When people see those letters behind your name, you have immediate credibility. No more questions are asked about your competence. The degree speaks for itself. Most (but not all) of their assumptions about you are thrown out the window, and they become willing to listen to you. I personally enjoy the stature that comes with my medical credentials.

In all honesty, as a black man in America, it's nice to have instant credibility when I put on my white coat, because when I'm not wearing it, it's a completely different story. As a young adult, I often felt as though nobody was listening to me about topics at hand. I've always been a thinker, but I thought nobody gave me a chance to truly express my opinions. Their assumption was that I only knew basketball. Now, the fact that I have a couple of letters after my name leads people to believe I'm an expert. Nobody questions my aptitude anymore. They understand that becoming a doctor requires something special, and those with medical degrees must have it.

Prime example. During my residency training, I considered going to graduate school for an MBA. There was one program, a very prestigious one, that I was considering. When I sent them an email to inquire, they basically told me my application was as good as accepted. My GMAT was waived, and all I needed to do was come interview, then submit the application.

At the interview, I was asked, "Isn't getting this MBA going to be trivial for you? You take care of dying people. Why would you want to do this? Finding ways to make money seems meaningless compared to what you do." Just because of my degree, they assumed I would thrive in their program. Furthermore, my interviewer assumed that I would not be stimulated and challenged. His inaccurate assessment of me (and of the meaning of business) was a result of the stature he attributed based on my academic credentials.

And this isn't unique to me; it's a general theme for medical doctors pursuing business degrees. Simply being a medical doctor opens all sorts of doors for you.

Allow me to interject a brief word of caution. This extreme level of respect and stature makes some physicians falsely believe they are higher than God Almighty. I am not advocating for that, and my hope is that you raise children who practice nobility and humility.

Among the most noble of physicians was Saint Luke. A companion to the apostle Paul, he exemplified the finest of character traits—traits all doctors should strive for. Like many physicians, Dr. Luke was multitalented. Aside from his medical practice, he was also a historian, having penned two books in the Bible, and an artist. While he had much to brag about, he never did. Dr. Luke was a humble man. In his writings, not once does he make note of himself in any fashion for gain. There he was, documenting the greatest events in the history of humankind, and he completely left himself out. And on the contrary, his entire purpose was to document the good works of other people. Had it not been for the writings of the apostle Paul, we wouldn't even know that Luke was a doctor. He clearly takes the back seat and allows others to shine.

Do you want your future physician to be humble? Are you humble? Is your child humble? Doctors are accomplished individuals, and it's very easy to reach into the bag of accolades to remind others of that. Confidence is good, pride is bad. Proud people have a difficult time listening to others. When caring for patients, it's essential that you pay attention to what they have to say. Here's a prime example:

Dr. Proud is an emergency room physician who has been practicing medicine for twenty-five years. She graduated from medical school, then matriculated into the number one emergency medicine training program in the country. She's not just good, she's really good!

Mr. Sick comes to the emergency department complaining of chest pain. "Dr. Proud," he says, "three hours ago my chest started hurting, and I couldn't breathe well." He points to the bottom of his breastbone. "The pain is right here."

"Oh," Dr. Proud says, "I've seen this a million times. You're having a heart attack. Just sit right there as we'll get things going for you as quickly as possible." She then turns to the computer and begins to write orders for medications and tests. "You'll need some aspirin immediately and an EKG to look at the electricity in your heart."

Five minutes later, the EKG is completed. "Yep, just as I thought, you've got what we call a STEMI. That's a really bad heart attack. We need to get you some clot-busting medicine stat so your entire heart doesn't die on us. Don't worry though, like I said, I've seen this a million times." Dr. Proud finishes placing a couple more orders, then stands up to leave.

"Wait!" Mr. Sick blurts out. "I needed to tell you about some other pains I'm having. I've read about this type of pain online, and I think it might be something else. You see, the pain also…"

"No need," Dr. Proud interrupts. "I've seen this…"

"Yes, I know…'a million times.' Okay, I'm trusting you."

The nurse walks into the room and sets up the clot-busting medication to run through Mr. Sick's IV. One hour later, his vital signs alarms are sounding off like police sirens. Within a matter of minutes, Mr. Sick is dead.

What Mr. Sick wanted to tell Dr. Proud was that the pain was also shooting straight into his back and across his shoulder blades. He was having an aortic dissection, which means his aorta (the largest artery in your body) had ripped open and blood was escaping. What further complicated this was the fact that Dr. Proud gave a clot buster, which made the bleeding significantly worse. Had Dr. Humble been present, she would have listened to the rest of Mr. Sick's story and easily identified the problem.

Okay, if you're over the age of thirty and just read that example, let me stop you right there. I know you're thinking about the chest pain you've had in the past, and about 50 percent of you are probably having chest pain right now. Calm down, it's okay. Just breathe. This isn't that common of a thing to happen. If you are truly concerned, go see your doctor.

Teach your children to be humble. This is a necessary trait of great physicians. The ability to listen to the patient is essential. The ability to say I don't know, then seek help is essential. The ability to make your team feel more important than you is essential. Humility is the heart of sustained success in any field; however, it is of special importance when taking care of someone else's life. If you've never considered this, now would be a great time to ask yourself a simple question: What am I doing to teach my child humility?

Matt Chandler does an excellent job teaching his children to be humble. He is a pastor in the Dallas, Texas, area. Some years back, my wife and I adopted his practice of apologizing and confessing to our children when we are in the wrong. In my household, it is mandatory for everyone, Mom and Dad included, to apologize when at fault. No exemptions.

"Sorry, Tony, I shouldn't have yelled at you. Instead of

assuming that you were the one who threw the ball through the patio door and shattered the glass, I should have asked you first. Daddy makes mistakes too and Daddy was wrong. Do you forgive me?"

In modeling this, my children are learning that it's okay to place yourself in vulnerable positions because they are only temporary. Yes, for a few seconds Tony has the upper hand and gets to decide if he will forgive me or not (and of course he always does), but as soon as that time passes, Daddy is 100 percent on top again. This also teaches him not to mistake humility for weakness.

Another simple way to begin instilling humility in your children is to make them serve others and teach them that there is no such thing as menial work. As an undergraduate student, like many of my now-doctor colleagues, I performed extremely well in a variety of arenas. In doing so, I built a reputation of excellence, and many students developed a certain level of respect for me. I became a mentor and role model to many who came after me. In a sense, I was untouchable when it came to academics and extracurricular activities. My confidence (not cockiness) was through the roof, and I needed to be put in check.

For over two years, I worked as a mentor in an office led by Drs. Linda Blockus and Susan Renoe. One day, out of the blue, Dr. Renoe told me to pick up the window cleaner and grab some paper towels. She was sitting comfortably at her computer, just rrelaxing, when she uttered her craziest words ever, "Go clean those windows, Dale."

This lady must have lost her mind, I thought. *She thinks I'm about to go clean those windows. Ha. Not happening. They don't pay me to do that.*

After a few uncomfortable seconds of staring, she hadn't retracted her command. "Dale," she said, "don't ever think you're too good to do anything. Stay humble."

Immediately, I got it. At that moment, I knew she was teaching me more than how to use Windex. I stood up, grabbed the cleaners, and waxed on, then waxed off. That lesson has never left me, and I teach my kids the same exact thing. Sure, stature is great, and you should desire this for your children, but without humility, it is dangerous!

The Love of Money

Yes, stature is the primary motive for most parent's desire to have physician children, but not far behind that comes the money. This is confounded by the reality that money can raise one's stature. Still, beyond that, the money alone is a desirable benefit. It's no secret that medical doctors are paid well. Year after year we top the list of highest-paid professions. As a matter of fact, I can't think of a single physician who has completed training and is working full-time who makes below six figures. Family medicine, pediatric medicine, and psychiatric medicine tend to have the lowest salaries in the medical world, yet according to a Merritt Hawkins and Associates report, even these "low"-paying specialties earn near $200,000 annually ($189,000 in the report). All those years of training lead to a nice little salary at the end of the day, and that's a perk that most parents want for their kids.

But Dr. Dale, you say, it's not about the money. Money is the root of all evil. Parents shouldn't want their children to chase this evilness.

My response to you is this; "That's foolishness!"

Of course, money plays a role in our decisions to pursue this career. Money is simply a tool meant to acquire resources for good use. It is the love of money that is "the root of all evil" (1 Timothy 6:10), not money in and of itself. Personally,

I have absolutely no qualms about teaching my children how to make a lot of money, and I strongly advise you to do the same. In America, pursuing a career in medicine is one of the most reliable ways to go about it. The key, however, is teaching them not to love it.

When your baby becomes a doctor, she'll be able to live a life that few people can. Foreign luxury cars, large homes, and expensive vacations aren't unusual among physicians. Many doctors easily spend five if not six figures on such things each year. We can afford to send our children to the nicest schools, become members of exclusive golf clubs, and enjoy the finest arts and culture available. I'd be lying to you if I said it's not an amazing lifestyle. What parent wouldn't want this for their children? And before you go on your guilt trip again, let me remind you that it's okay for you to desire wealth for your children. There is nothing wrong with that.

While we're on the topic of money, allow me to provide another statement of caution. Teach your children, starting now, what medical schools don't: how to save and invest money. Also, if you haven't done so, I encourage you to read *The Millionaire Next Door* by Thomas Stanley and William Danko. A physician mentor of mine (who is worth over $20 million) recommended it to me, and it completely changed my financial perspective.

The authors of *The Millionaire Next Door* do an excellent job distinguishing between high income and high wealth. Doctors tend to be high income, not necessarily high wealth. Income is the money you bring home while wealth, on the other hand, is the worth of your possessions. According to their research, physicians tend to under accumulate wealth. This means that even though we have those large paychecks, apparently, we don't know what to do with them. Stanley and Danko attribute this issue in part to society's pressure on doctors to live the flashy lifestyle I described earlier. Even though most of us are not millionaires, when our high social status confounds our economic status, the result is excessive spending beyond our means. This is a very easy trap for physicians to fall into, and something you should be cautioning your children about now.

Here's how the trap works. Your child is sold the dream of becoming rich by being a medical doctor. As a matter of fact, society at large is sold that dream. But here's what the dream sellers conveniently leave out: the opportunity cost and the debt of becoming a medical doctor.

When I graduated college at the age of twenty-one, many of my friends immediately joined the workforce. I remember hearing their salaries and asking myself why I was taking out loans to get more education. Those in engineering were starting out making over $70,000 a year. At twenty-something years old, you don't have many major expenses. This allows you to buy what you need and throw the rest into an IRAs or a 401K! For fourteen years I was so focused on completing my medical training that I didn't pay any attention to financial planning. In order for me to catch up to the wealth of my college buddies by age sixty-five, I'll have to invest over double what they do since they had a ten-year head start. Ten years might not sound like much, but when you account for compounding interest, that financial difference adds up. This is the opportunity cost we, as physicians, pay.

The second thing to keep in mind is that medical school isn't cheap. Oh, and somebody has to pay for it. That somebody is typically the person getting the degree. I'll keep it real with you. I'm not the slightest bit wealthy. Janai and I have debt on top of debt on top of debt. The average medical student comes out with over $150,000 worth of educational debt. Please note, I said average. That means that there are a lot of students with much more than that. By the time they start practicing as fully licensed physicians, their loans are as much as a mortgage on a decent-size house.

Furthermore, beyond the debt, everyone wants a piece of their paychecks. Uncle Sam takes his cut, various medical societies take theirs, and professional licensing boards grab their share too. At the end of the day, the take home is a lot less than some might think (but not that much less to make it not worth it).

I don't mean to frighten you off, but I do want you to be aware of these realities. Yes, doctors make a lot of money, but for a variety of reasons, many doctors are not actually wealthy. Knowing this, I strongly encourage you to start teaching your children how to manage money from day one. Whether they become doctors or not, this is essential to their future success.

Other than being proud of your child and excited about all the perks he or she will have as a physician, there's another reason why it makes you feel good to say, "My baby's a doctor." Come on, you know what I'm talking about. It makes you feel good because it reflects the type of parent you are. Nobody becomes a doctor without help, and that help usually begins at home with the parents.

When people learn that my parents raised two medical doctors, a lawyer, and a vice president of a publicly traded company, their response is, "Well done. How did you do that?" The success of the children is a greater success of the parents. I'm reminded of a biblical passage in which Jesus tells his disciples they will go on to do greater works than He did. That's the true mark of a leader—when those you lead can grow to do more than you did. Parents who raise a doctor should be proud of their efforts and accomplishment.

So, why do you want your child to become a doctor? Are there other reasons beyond what I have stated above? I certainly do hope so. Stature, fame, money—those are all great things, but medicine is so much more than that. There is so much more to what we do and who we are than what society portrays.

One day, when you say, "My baby's a doctor," I want you to be proud, not because of how other people will then view you and your child, but because of who your son or daughter has become. It's not the MD, DO, or Ph.D. that matters—it's the name in front of those letters. Those who can endure medical training have amazing potential to impact lives for the better. Be proud of that!

PART 2

Character Matters

4

THE GOOD DOCTOR

Knowledge will give you power. But character, respect.

—Bruce Lee

On May 15, 2010, I became a medical doctor. I remember the day as if it were yesterday. Standing in Jesse Auditorium at the University of Missouri, I noticed that hundreds of eyes were fixed upon ninety some odd students. Together, as a class of new physicians, we recited this oath, which is held in the highest regard among all professions:

> I swear to fulfill, to the best of my ability and judgment, this covenant:
> I will respect the hard-won scientific gains of those physicians in whose steps I walk, and gladly share such knowledge as is mine with those who are to follow. I will apply, for the benefit of the sick, all measures which are required, avoiding those twin traps of overtreatment and therapeutic nihilism. I will remember that there is art to medicine as well as science, and that warmth, sympathy, and understanding may outweigh the surgeon's knife or

the chemist's drug. I will not be ashamed to say "I know not," nor will I fail to call in my colleagues when the skills of another are needed for a patient's recovery. I will respect the privacy of my patients, for their problems are not disclosed to me that the world may know. Most especially must I tread with care in matters of life and death. If it is given me to save a life, all thanks. But it may also be within my power to take a life; this awesome responsibility must be faced with great humbleness and awareness of my own frailty. Above all, I must not play at God. I will remember that I don't treat a fever chart, a cancerous growth, but a sick human being, whose illness may affect the person's family and economic stability. My responsibility includes these related problems, if I am to care adequately for the sick. I will prevent disease whenever I can, for prevention is preferable to cure. I will remember that I remain a member of society, with special obligations to all my fellow human beings, those sound of mind and body as well as the infirm. If I don't violate this oath, may I enjoy life and art, respected while I live and remembered with affection thereafter. May I always act so as to preserve the finest traditions of my calling and may I long experience the joy of healing those who seek my help.

That was a very special day for me. My dream had become a reality, and it was clear that I had joined something much larger than myself. I was now a member of one of the most noble professions since the creation of humankind. Those in the medical field live a life of servitude and are called to the highest level of responsibility. Since the dawn of the profession, some of society's best and brightest have sought to care for human life: physically, emotionally, and spiritually. They have committed themselves to putting forth 100 percent effort at all times, never relenting. When the life of another human is entrusted to you, excellence is demanded. That's what being a doctor is all about—giving your all for the good of others.

Consider the importance of what we loosely call the Hippocratic oath (I say *loosely* because many institutions use a modified or entirely different oath). Every doctor graduating from a medical school in the United States is to recite this upon graduation. Similar to being sworn into a fraternity, this is a powerful statement of commitment to do your best at all cost, to respect the craft of medicine, and to treat others in the highest regard. It signifies your induction into a special brotherhood. Every doctor understands the perils that were overcome to gain the honor of wearing the white coat, and the Hippocratic oath serves to remind us of that throughout our entire careers.

My intent in writing this book is not simply for you to gain pointers to get your kid into medical school (and yes, I will give you many of those as we progress). That's too easy, and in all honesty, it's not worth my time. If that were the goal, I'd just direct you to some basic cookbook resources that walk you through the process step by step. Many such books exist and can be found at your local bookstore. But that's not what this book is about, nor is it what I'm about. Rather, I intend to show you how to raise an ideal physician, one who is above reproach.

What society needs are leaders who are willing to do what's right regardless of the consequences—those who hold themselves accountable to a high moral standard not dictated by the fads of their day, but rather by their convictions of truth. We need doctors who do their best, every day, to live out the oath they professed at the initiation of their careers.

If you're going to raise a doctor, raise one like that! But to do so, you must first appreciate the fact that excellence is emitted from within. If you properly train your child's mind and heart, this training will be revealed in his or her behavior.

Three Character Traits That Rig the Deck in Favor of Your Child

As I spoke with parents during the writing of this book, one thing was definite: In raising their children, their main focus wasn't academics. Something else superseded that. The majority of them emphasized the importance they placed on developing their children's character. When asked how they raised a doctor, their answers weren't focused on math, science, or literature. Rather, they were all focused on disciplines of thought, perception, and action. Once these things have been established, the intellectual components naturally follow. To these parents, it was crystal clear that if you want to raise a doctor, you must start with the character of your child.

The things we believe determine how we behave. This behavior is the phenotype of our character and is derived from our morals. Right versus wrong. Good versus bad. Just versus unjust. Every action in life will fall into one of those categories. None of us are perfect little angels. We all have actions on both sides of the column, but the key is to tip the balance in favor of the positive side, and when the stakes are high, always choose right. To raise an ideal physician, you must be intentional about this early in your child's life. As the parent, it's your duty to mold his or her character.

Research suggests that a child's character is established and fixed by as early as age six. The propensity to lie, cheat, and steal—all those things that seem so harmless in the toddler years—can stay with your child for the duration of his or her life. It is imperative that you identify the character traits you desire your child to have, and begin instilling these from day one. Your goal is to *rig the deck* in your child's favor, and your window of opportunity to get this right might be smaller than you realize.

Integrity

Although there are numerous character traits that we would love our doctors to have, there are three that I believe must be mastered at an early age. Integrity is the first of these. It's the starting point for all positive character traits. Integrity is the notion of valuing your values. I know that's a little confusing. All it means is that the actions you deem to be good in life are the ones you live by. Everyone knows it's bad to lie, yet people do it all the time. But people of integrity knows it's wrong to lie, so they don't.

Within the medical profession, integrity is the *most important* trait to possess. This is true because doctors can easily take advantage of their patients, and unfortunately some do just that. Where integrity lacks, all bets are off, and we enter a no-holds-barred situation. Our field is unique in that for all practical purposes, doctors are the suppliers and the consumers of the service.

> One of my favorite definitions of integrity is what you do when nobody looks. What do you do when nobody's looking?
> —DAVID S. TAYLOR, CEO OF PROCTOR & GAMBLE

"But Dr. Dale, my doctor didn't pay my last medical bills. I did. I'm the consumer!"

I understand that, but here's what I mean. When I care for critically ill patients, typically, they have absolutely no idea what I'm doing. At best, the nonmedically trained patient may understand 25 percent of the entire process, and that's being generous. There's a reason it took me fourteen years to complete my medical training, and we can't expect our patients to understand the full intricacies of their ailments. They rely on our expertise.

If I say drug X is the best drug to use, then that's what they want me to use. When I sign an order to have the patient do a specific type of therapy that costs thousands of dollars, for the most part, they agree without question. So, in the end, patients pay us for services that we tell them they need. We decide what they purchase. It's like walking into the car dealership, and the dealer tells you which car you're going to buy. Do you see how that can be a problem?

America depends on doctors of high integrity. The disproportion in knowledge between the supplier (doctor) and the true consumer (patient) is a major point of vulnerability. This is true on an individual as well as a global level. It has health implications, social implications, and of course financial implications. We need physicians who not only know what's right, but also do what's right! Medical schools appreciate this necessity as well, which is why they rely so heavily on letters of recommendation. The ultimate purpose of those letters is to help them determine if a student has this character trait.

There are tens of thousands of wonderful medical school applicants each year. Some of them have perfect grade point averages yet still don't get into medical school. Why is that? Often, it is because someone has questioned their intentions and actions. Their integrity has been challenged. Don't let that be the case with your child. Model integrity and offer constant reminders of its importance.

In his book *Very Influential People* (VIP), author O. S. Hawkins states, "People who influence others for good all have a common characteristic: they are men and women of impeccable integrity." As a caretaker of life, I believe the primary job of physicians is to influence others for good. This should be true physically, mentally, and morally. Hawkins further dissects the concept of integrity as follows: "Integrity is rooted in our private life. Integrity is reflected in our personal life. Integrity is reinforced in our professional life. And finally, integrity is revealed in our public life."

After reading this, I considered the implications of his short thesis. Parents are proficient at educating their kids pertaining to personal, professional, and public life; however, I am not certain this is true for the place where integrity is rooted: the private life. It is critical that we specifically train our children to always do the right things behind closed doors. This will help them attain a high standard of morality and self-worth.

Responsibility

If I had to choose one thing that helps me to perform at my highest level, it is knowing that I am responsible for the health of other people. Responsibility is the second character trait you must instill in your child. Unlike with integrity, you can't sneak your way into medical school without this one. All physicians have a certain level of responsibility, which made it possible for them to advance through the various academic phases of their medical education. The great thing about this trait is that it is among the easiest to teach a child. It can be practiced using all sorts of objects such as toys, clothes, and food. It can also be taught with simple activities. As a parent, it's your responsibility to teach your child about responsibility.

Responsibility is about two things: (1) acceptance and (2) accountability. The moment you accept anything, you become responsible for it. An object, a moment in time, a thought— all are things that a person can become responsible for. It is important to note that true responsibility cannot be given; one must accept it. Consider this scenario.

Let's say I am going out of town and forget to make arrangements for my dog, Checkers, to be watched. You know my puppy well and we're really good friends, so I know you'll be okay taking care of him. When I ask you to watch him, you tell me that you need to check your calendar and see what you're up to this weekend. Well, I've got to get out of town right away, so I drop him off at your front door with a thank-you note, then head off to the airport. Four hours later you call me and let me know that you had to fly out for a business meeting. By the time I get to my destination and buy another ticket to rush home and get Checkers, the poor dog is gone, leaving only his crate behind. Who was responsible for Checkers? I gave him to you to watch, but you never accepted. I was the one responsible for him.

When patients present to the hospital in critical condition, they never magically show up in my ICU. The typical evolution of the process is as follows: The patient presents to the emergency department (ED) because somebody recognized that something was not right. The ED staff assess the patient and do their best to stabilize him or her. When it is deemed that the patient is sick enough to require intensive care, I (or a delegated member or my team) am called to evaluate the patient to confirm the necessity of our care. We then have the authority to either accept this patient to come under our care, or to decline caring for the patient. When we decline, the patient's care has nothing to do with us. If the emergency room staff decides to send the patient to our ICU without our permission, they remain responsible for the care of that patient. But as soon as we accept the patient to come under our care, we become 100 percent responsible.

The second aspect of responsibility pertains to what you do with what you've accepted. This is accountability. Because you have accepted it, you can now be held liable for what happens to it. Doctors accept the role of being healthcare providers and in doing so become accountable for the healthcare they provide (or don't provide). When I tell the ED team that I'm accepting their patient to my team, I become accountable for his or her well-being. This accountability is not trivial, and is the reason patients are able to file outrageous malpractice claims against physicians.

In his writings, Dr. Luke documents a parable told by Jesus (see Luke 19:12–24). In it, a master leaves his servants with one gold coin each. His instructions are clear: "See what you can earn while I'm gone." None of the servants said, "No, I don't want this coin." They all accepted it. Upon his return, one of his servants had earned ten gold coins, another had earned five gold coins, and another had only the one coin given to him by his master. Pleased with the first servant, the master made him ruler over ten cities. Likewise, he made the second servant ruler over five cities. But when he heard that the third servant didn't earn anything, he took it as a sign of irresponsibility. "Take his one coin and give it to the servant with ten," he commanded.

As you rear your children in the discipline of responsibility, remember what Jesus said, "Whoever is faithful with very little will also be faithful with much, and whoever is dishonest with very little will also be dishonest with much" (Luke 16:10 BRB). Teach your children to be responsible for the little things, and with time, they'll be ready for the responsibility of caring for human life.

Grit

The third essential character of the ideal physician is grit. Hands down, this is one of my favorites. I absolutely love seeing the courage and resolve necessary to accomplish a goal. I get excited even writing about it.

Grit is the expression of an individual's passion. It is his or her love for a dream. It's what makes that boxer get off the ground to keep on fighting. It's the desire to win! Without a doubt, grit is necessary for physicians. Even before getting into medical school, it's needed to make it through the premedical years. After that, it's needed to get through medical school, and then residency training. Along this journey, there will be numerous obstacles and challenges that can easily derail one from pursuing the fight, whatever it may be. Those without grit will fail. Those who possess it will prevail!

In my role as a critical care physician, patients can die if I lose my grit. Difficult clinical cases require in-depth investigations and are often met with more negative results than positive. The ability of a doctor to repeatedly ask why, then seek the answer can be the difference between life and death. This insatiable persistence until resolution is the grit that excellent doctors possess. And students shouldn't wait until medical school to learn it.

I developed grit on the basketball court during my elementary days. Day in and day out, I played ball against older brothers, cousins, and friends. Since I wasn't gifted with height, the odds were stacked against me, as you can imagine. But God did gift me with grit, and the one thing I knew was that practice was the great equalizer. I might not have made it to the NBA, or even the collegiate level, but grit got me a decent reputation in one-on-one and rec ball. With time, I was able to beat many of my older and bigger competitors, simply because I had unparalleled determination.

I firmly believe in hard work, practice, competition, and the desire to win. My wife will be the first to tell you that I'm not one of those participation trophy dads, and I wasn't raised to give anything less than my best. Doctors are competitive people. It's not easy to consistently get the highest grades and be at the top of your class. It's not easy to excel in non-academic arenas, which medical schools look favorably upon. Although these things are challenging to accomplish, most doctors are driven by a desire to be excellent. To perform at this level, you must have grit.

Teach this to your children early, from day one. And don't just take my word for it. Ask any of the doctors' parents I spoke with during the writing of this book, and they'll tell you the same.

Remember earlier when I said that you must "rig the deck" in favor of your child? That stands for Responsibility, Integrity, and Grit. These are three essential characteristics that parents should hone and encourage if they desire to have professionally successful children. So **RIG** the deck!

The Doctor

In 1891, a painting titled *The Doctor* was publicly exhibited. This famous piece of art was painted by Sir Luke Fildes. In it, a child lays limp and pale on a bed. A father stands concerned in the distance next to his distraught wife, who is sitting with her face tucked away on the table. The last person in this masterpiece, the doctor, stares intensely, perplexedly, and most important, lovingly at the child. For me, what makes this

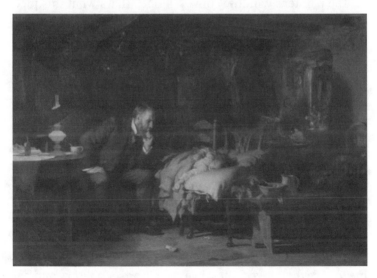

painting interesting is that this doctor has no tools. There are no fancy stethoscopes, reflex hammers, or otoscopes. All he has to offer is himself.

This painting was inspired by the death of Fildes's son some years earlier. A physician by the name of Dr. Murray came to their home and attended to the sick child. Unfortunately, the young boy died, but Fildes never forgot the feeling he had when Dr. Murray arrived at his home. He always remembered the compassion showed by this expert physician.

Many people look at this painting and immediately focus on the physician; however, the true focus is the window. "At the cottage window," Fildes would write, "the dawn begins to steal in—the dawn that is the critical time of all deadly illnesses—and with it the parents again take hope into their hearts, the mother hiding her face to escape giving vent to her emotion, the father laying his hand on the shoulder of his wife in encouragement of the first glimmerings of the joy which is to follow."

The painter's window conveys hope. That's what this piece is about. Fildes's work illustrates the true power of a physician: the ability to provide hope.

> *I always knew I wanted to be a doctor,*
> *but I also knew that being a doctor meant more*
> *than treating just the patient in front of you.*
> —RISA LAVIZZO-MOUREY, MD, FORMER CEO OF THE
> ROBERT WOOD JOHNSON FOUNDATION

Hope is one of the strongest feelings that humans can express. As an ICU physician, the worst part of my job is seeing people die. Not infrequently, friends and family plead with me to save their loved ones. I've seen more people cry and collapse than I can count. It's reached the point that I no longer know how to describe the emotion I feel during these times of helplessness. It hurts, but I have to accept the reality of these situations. At that point in time, the best thing I can do for any family is to tell them the truth.

Critical care doctors are not asked to treat healthy people. If you're my patient in the hospital, that often means things aren't just bad—they are very bad. And in those situations, the deck is stacked against you. But here's where that hope comes into play, and why I love my job: No matter what I say to a patient or family, when they see me, it ignites an amazing hope in their eyes. They hope we have a diagnosis. They hope we can treat the illness. They hope things are getting better. I'd dare say that besides the faith they put in their personal Savior, they've never experienced a greater hope. By the very nature of our jobs, physicians provide hope beyond comprehension.

When patients see us, it's either going to be good news or bad news. They hope for the former. It's not that we all want this responsibility—and trust me, it's a very big responsibility—but we accept it and are accountable for it. I love carrying this weight, because I understand how much that hope means to the patient and family. It's an honor to experience it with them, no matter what the patient's outcome is.

During my fourth year of medical school, I did an elective rotation in Galveston. While on the general medicine inpatient team, I helped to take care of a dying man who had a dear and loving wife. She was with her husband every day and never wanted to leave his side. Religiously, she would profess that he was going to live. "Not my husband," she'd say. "It's not his time. We're walking out of this hospital together."

As much as I wanted that to happen for her, other than a direct miracle from Jesus, which I do believe can happen, there was no way this patient was going to survive. When I told this wife that her husband likely wouldn't leave the hospital alive, she was in utter dismay and distress. The interesting thing, however, is that her faith in us, the healthcare providers, only grew stronger. Her hope in God delivering a miracle through our hands was palpable.

I recall a touching moment we shared one day. Our medical team was having a conversation with her, and she didn't seem to be paying much attention. Suddenly, she looked straight in my eyes as hers watered with tears, "Oh, I see," she said lovingly. "You're an angel. God sent you down from heaven for us. You're an angel, aren't you?"

As much as I wanted to be her angel and deliver new life from God to her husband, that wasn't the Lord's will. I hate it that we couldn't save his life, but there is only so much we can do as humans. Although it hurt me to see his wife and children go through the cycle of hope then despair, it was a noble honor to walk the journey with her. I was glad to be her light in a dark place. This is perhaps the most important role of the physician: *to be the bearer of light and hope.* It's exactly what Sir Luke Fildes was depicting in his painting. The touch of light shining through the cottage window is the hope we, as physicians, must provide our patients. As a parent, you too should encourage your child to bear hope.

Hope is distributed by optimistic people. In my capacity as a mentor, I speak with students who are under too much pressure from their family. "You must be a doctor," they're told. "You'll never become a doctor if you're not the number one student in your class. You'll never be a successful doctor if you don't publish a paper." These students are approached from a negative and pessimistic perspective. This modeling of behavior will carry on to the way they deliver care to their patients. If this is the way you converse with people, especially those you expect to become future doctors, then stop it! Optimism nurtures the gift of hope, and this is essential to practicing good medicine.

The training of a physician begins at birth, not in medical school. Hone a mindset of humble determination and success in your future doctor. Achievement begins within, and when raising a good doctor, it's the duty of the parent to foster this.

PARENT PERSPECTIVE

Sports & Integrity

I have always instilled in my children that one of the most important virtues to maintain throughout your life is your integrity. I would often say: "You walk in with your integrity and you leave with it." To teach them this important lesson, I enrolled them in sports.

All of my children were encouraged to sign up for many sports. I was not concerned about their athletic ability, but more about how these team activities would build their morals. I emphasized the importance of playing well with the team over that of winning. In sports, everyone wants to win; however, it takes honesty to maintain respect. I encouraged them to treat everyone fairly and that their character was more important than being popular or a superstar athlete. The values I taught my children focused on not putting success above integrity.

My son, for example, gave up his playing time in basketball, to allow another player, who mostly sat on the bench, to also benefit from the full sports experience. He could have taken all the glory; but, instead, he voiced to the coaches that he felt this was wrong. He chose to do what he believed was fair. He was willing to accept a loss to maintain his moral character. Because of this, losing was no longer foreign to him and he could weather the small losses that would come in his career while succeeding in the grand scheme.

Participating in sports mirrors life experiences, especially when it comes to integrity. By enrolling my children into organized sports; I was teaching them the importance of this concept. I continue to tell my daughter, a soon-to-be cardiologist, that you must be a patient advocate regardless of how it affects your own success; and maintaining your integrity is front and center in doing that.

VIRGINIA D. BANKS, MD, MBA
Mother of Dr. Mary Branch

5

GREAT EXPECTATIONS

High expectations are the key to everything.

—Sam Walton

I must have been in the second or third grade when my dad did something that would forever change the way I approached life. One day, I came home from school ecstatic. Everything was going right, and I was on cloud nine. I had a test that day and performed extremely well. Back then, I did okay in school, but I wasn't the straight A student that I would later become. I waited patiently for Papa to get home from work, and when he did, I proudly approached him.

"Papa," I said, "I got a 98 percent on that exam today!" Standing quietly, I prepared myself for a "good job, Son," "atta-boy," or what would have been the best of them all: "Let's go get some ice cream to celebrate."

But none of those was his response. Instead, Papa looked up and asked, "What happened to the other two points?"

Really, Dad! What happened to the other two points?

It's not that he was unhappy—he just wanted to know what exactly I needed to learn in order to get all the questions right. Why aim for a 98 percent if you can shoot for 100 percent? If you can't tell, Papa doesn't mess around. He has always had extremely high expectations for his children.

My survey of doctors' parents showed a theme consistent with my dad's perspective. These parents tended to set high but reasonable expectations. Given the type A personalities of many physicians, I am not surprised by this at all. High expectations are necessary in the field of medicine.

I myself am a pulmonary and critical care physician. This means that I often take care of the sickest patients in the hospital. My patients and their families don't want me to get it 98 percent correct; they want me to score 100 percent every single time. That 2 percent isn't trivial, and they're literally betting their lives that I get it right!

As doctors, we know our patients have high expectations for us. Actually, they have extremely high expectations. Thankfully, we are often able to meet them because our parents had even higher expectations. And the interesting thing about that is, they did it intentionally to prepare us for what was to come.

There is a school of thought that is rather bothersome to me. Individuals who subscribe to it believe that expectations should not be placed on children because "expectations are the source of disappointments." When a child is expected to win a basketball game, but doesn't, everyone feels bad. Instead of telling our children what is expected of them, we should allow them freedom in their desires and cheer them along simply for doing the best that they can. Everyone gets a participation trophy. I completely agree that we should support our sons and daughters for giving their all; however, the problem arises in that we never really know when someone is giving their all.

When I was about eight years old, I attended a summer basketball camp hosted by Avery Johnson, who at that time was the star NBA point guard of the San Antonio Spurs. I remember hundreds of us sitting on the ground when Avery picked out a kid who would have been about fifteen years old.

"I want you to run as fast as you can from here to there," Avery instructed him.

The young man responded with an affirmative nod, indicating that he was willing and able to do that.

Avery gave him a pat on the back. "Give it your all. On your mark, get set, go!"

Like lightning, this kid jetted across the gym while Avery timed him.

"8.32 seconds! Very good! Did you run your fastest?"

The kid nodded yes.

Then Avery took out a twenty-dollar bill and told the young man, "If you can beat that time, this twenty is yours. On your mark, get set, go!"

Now he was really running. That young man zipped down the court and back as if his life was depending on it.

Avery smiled. "7.92. Come get your twenty."

> *Success is not what you have done compared to what others have done. Success is what you have done compared to what you were supposed to do.*
>
> —TONY EVANS, SENIOR PASTOR OF
> OAK CLIFF BIBLE FELLOWSHIP

We all thought that young man had given it his all the first time, and he thought so too. But see how easily he beat the former time? Avery provided him with an incentive, expecting him to run faster, and he did just that! In doing so, that gentleman showed us he really hadn't done his best.

This is the exact problem with parents believing it's okay to not set expectations "as long as the child does his or her best." You never really know what that child's best is if there is no bar to strive for. In my household, we accept participation trophies, but they come with a clear message to my children that in the real world, not everybody gets one. Awards are earned.

Pygmalion Proof

"You see, really and truly, apart from the things anyone can pick up (the dressing and the proper way of speaking, and so on), the difference between a lady and a flower girl is not how she behaves, but how she's treated. I shall always be a flower girl to Professor Higgins, because he always treats me as a flower girl, and always will; but I know I can be a lady to you, because you always treat me as a lady, and always will."

—George Bernard Shaw, Pygmalion

Expectations matter! This isn't theory; decades of research have shown us this. In 1968, Robert Rosenthal and Lenore Jacobson published the book *Pygmalion in the Classroom.* The title was borrowed from George Bernard Shaw's play *Pygmalion.* These researchers were determined to know if other people's expectations could affect an individual's outcomes. More specifically, they wanted to know how the expectations of teachers affected student outcomes.

To find out, they conducted a study in which students at a school were all given an IQ test. The catch, however, was that nobody was told it was an IQ test. Instead, Rosenthal and Jacobson mislead the teachers by titling the test the "Harvard Test of Inflected Acquisition." The teachers were led to believe the test would accurately identify students who were on the verge of having a dramatic increase in their IQ. The researchers then chose students at random and told the teachers these students had been identified as those who were about to bloom with a rapid increase intellectual ability. Supposedly, these students had a tremendous amount of potential as evidenced by the test. In reality, the only known differences between the students in this study were the teachers' new perceptions of their potential.

After following the students for two years, Rosenthal and Jacobson found that the students whose teachers were led to believe they would have higher IQ gains did, in fact, have those gains. These same students were also described in more positive ways than students who were not in that fabricated category.

Why did the students who were falsely identified as having more potential end up doing better? The answer is simple: because of higher expectations! The teachers had higher expectations for the children simply because they were told these select students had more potential. That's it. Nothing else suggested that. In believing this fabrication, the teachers then subconsciously set expectations on themselves to ensure those students did well. If the students performed poorly, the blame could be placed on the teachers since "everyone" knew these key students were supposed to do well. This results in more time given to those students to answer questions before going to the next student, gently correcting those students, redirecting them to the right answer instead of just moving along, and more feedback to their parents.

When you consider the implications of Rosenthal and Jacobson's findings, it's pretty scary. Not only am I telling you that your own expectations of your child matter, but the expectations other people have on your child matter as well.

So how can we determine their expectations on our kids? It's true that we can't control what others think, but we can influence it. It's your job to make sure others expect your child to be great! There are two simple ways to do this.

First, make it clear to your child that you are expecting greatness from him or her. If you're not expecting this, don't think for a second that anyone else will. Your child needs to get this from home before they can accept it from outside. Furthermore, once he or she understands Mommy and Daddy's high standards, your child will exude that—and others will pick up on it. Teachers and coaches will reset their expectation gauge to a higher level. In doing so, they also reset the gauge for how much stake they have in your child's success.

The second way to make sure other people have high expectations of your child is by being a constant presence in your son or daughter's life and telling others about these expectations. It's one thing to tell someone you expect greatness of your child, but it comes through much louder when they see you constantly pouring into your child to ensure their success. You should take the guesswork out of it for the teachers. Subconsciously, they are wanting to know which parents are most invested. If they constantly see you, and you directly tell them what your expectations of your child are, most teachers will do their best to help you meet those expectations.

It Starts with You

Expectations are foundational to your children's successes, and you—yes, you—are responsible for making them known. Let me be clear: This is imperative for development, and you should be intentional about it! For us, as parents, to do this, we must first know what an expectation is. To expect something is to deem it likely to occur. In common vernacular, we often misuse the word *expectation*. Parents say they have expectations for their children when what they really have are rules. Consider this scenario:

Johnny is a "difficult" child and always gets in trouble. Every time his parents go out, he has a party and trashes the place. One night, as his parents are leaving, they say, "Johnny, we're going out this evening. These are our expectations of you: No partying, clean up after yourself, and in bed by midnight."

Are those really expectations? No, they are not.

What they were really saying was, "Johnny, here are your rules for the night."

How could they consider these three items to be expectations if expectations are things that are likely to occur? Knowing Johnny's history and behavioral trends, he doesn't sound like the type of child who will abide by those standards. Johnny's parents have done nothing to make him more likely to adhere to their rules. In order to have an expectation of someone, you must first believe that person is capable of achieving it, and second, he or she must be willing to try to achieve it.

As parents, we have zero right to expect anything of our children if we haven't empowered them to achieve it. The expectations we put on our children require that we place even greater expectations on ourselves. It all starts with us, not our children!

My son Tony knows that when he comes home from school, he is to change his clothes, do his math, then help teach his younger brother how to count. I can expect these tasks of him because his mother and I have trained him to the point that he is capable of accomplishing them. We've spent countless hours doing the math problems with him. We've repeatedly shown him how to take off his clothes and where to put them. He's watched us review numbers with his younger brother, then practiced doing the same after we finished. We've empowered him pertaining to these particular tasks. If we hadn't, we couldn't expect him to do it on his own, could we? He wouldn't know how.

The second requirement of an expectation is the desire of the individual to accomplish the task. You cannot expect anything of your child if he or she isn't trying to do it. If you know your daughter doesn't want to do something, why would you ever think she would be likely to do it? One might argue that children don't desire to eat broccoli. But what most children do desire is to please their parents; therefore, they will eat the broccoli if trained and properly instructed. Or perhaps, they just want the desert that comes as a result of eating their dinner in its entirety. There are many reasons children might want to do something; at least one of them is necessary for you to set an expectation of them accomplishing it.

In appreciating these two requirements for placing expectations upon our children (capability and desire/effort), we can understand why to expect things of our children is to expect even greater things of ourselves. With each expectation you place on them, you add extra responsibility to yourself. If you expect them to make straight A's, it is your duty to train them to the point that they are capable of making straight A's and to motivate them so they desire to do so. It would be asinine of us as parents to place any expectation on our children without doing our part of preparing them ahead of time.

Children Live Up to High Expectations

The parents I surveyed didn't say that they placed expectations on their children; rather, they placed *high* expectations on their children. *High* is the key word. Asking your son to make 100 percent on a test instead of 98 percent is a high expectation. Yet it's still reasonable. If you can score a 98 percent, you can probably score a 100 percent. Raising a doctor requires you to train your child to do things that most other children either can't or won't do. This is the qualifier for a high expectation. If everyone else could do it, then it would just be an average expectation, and that wouldn't put your child ahead of the pack.

Something else we know is that students are very good at meeting expectations. In 2015, I had the honor of being the first ever "College Signing Day" keynote speaker for the Townview School of Engineering and Math (SEM). When I got the invite, I was relatively new to the Dallas area and had never heard of the school. The more I asked about SEM, the more I was impressed. These were just a few of their accolades:

- Number one in Texas Best Public Schools list

- Number three in the *Washington Post*'s America's Most Challenging High Schools list

- Number three in *U.S. News & World Report*'s Best High Schools list

- Ranked number one in the world for mathematics

These kids were smart, and I knew I had to step my speaking game up to deliver something of value to them.

In anticipation of my big day speaking at SEM, I mapped my route to the school and realized it was in South Dallas. For my non-Texan readers, south Dallas is what some people would consider the other side of the tracks. This immediately piqued my interest! Who were these south Dallas students laying the academic smackdown on the rest of the world?

I arrived that day to see a school full of Hispanic and Black teenagers. Most people would have been surprised to see that. *Minority kids can't perform that well, can they? Something must be wrong! They're cheating!* It's this foolish mindset of low expectations that leads to underperformance in low-income areas. What SEM proves is that high expectations don't just matter—they're essential for success.

That day, I had the chance to speak with Dr. Tiffany Huitt, who was the school's principal. I asked her if these students were bussed in from more affluent areas in the Dallas metroplex. Were they able to perform well because they had access to the resources necessary to thrive? Her answer was an emphatic no. Those students lived in West and South Dallas. No more or no less resources than all the other kids from that side of the tracks.

My next question was, "How do you do it? How do you get them to perform so well?" Please keep in mind that I wasn't just asking how she got these kids to perform at status quo or just above average. What I was asking was how did she get them to become some of the top performers in the entire world. Her response was very simple, "If you give them the tools they need and set high expectations, they'll meet them."

A self-fulfilling prophecy is a prediction that comes to fruition due to a positive feedback loop between your beliefs and behaviors. Consider Dr. Huitt's statement again: "If you give them the tools they need and set high expectations, they'll meet them." Do you see how that became a self-fulfilling prophecy for her and her students? Here's a little secret about high expectations: they work because they are the genesis for such prophecies.

Case in point. If you have young children, you're reading this book because you want them to be successful and you have high expectations. These high expectations have led you to pick up this book, which in turn will provide you with beneficial information and perspective to give your children an advantage over others. Your behavior in acquiring and reading this book is the evidence that you believe your expectations will become reality. And they will become reality because you are working to make it so. This is a self-fulfilling prophecy, triggered by your high expectations.

Les Brown is one of the world's foremost motivational speakers. He has a saying I love: "Wants show up in conversation, expectations show up in behavior." In life, most people want great things. You want a Range Rover. You want a wonderful marriage. You want to be liked by other people. That's all perfectly fine; there's nothing wrong with wanting these things. What bothers me, however, is when people express their many wants, then mope around complaining of all that they lack.

Remember, "wants show up in conversation, expectations show up in behavior." These same people that mope around town and filibuster about their wants don't have behaviors consistent with their desires. You want a Range Rover, but you're not working any harder to save the money. You want a good marriage, but you don't make the time to date your spouse or even get home at a reasonable hour. You want people to like you, but you never offer yourself to do favors. Your behaviors aren't in line with your wants. Because this is so, I know you don't expect to receive these things. If you do, you're delusional.

Parents must remember that their children's success will be the result of the parents' beliefs and behaviors, which subsequently will translate into met expectations. In raising a doctor, your expectations should be consistent with the expectations of medical school admission committees as well as the expectations of patients. Your goal is to ensure that the early stage expectations you set for your children are high enough to prepare them to meet and exceed the expectations they will face along their premedical and medical journeys (in part 3 of this book, we'll address some of this by covering what medical schools are looking for in applicants).

The Paycheck

Dr. Jared Davis is a good friend of mine. I met him when we were young and eager medical students. He attended Meharry Medical College, which is the same school my wife graduated from. Jared is one of the most determined individuals I know. From the first day I met him, it was clear that his high aspirations and expectations would come to pass. Today, he has almost completed his plastic surgery training and is simultaneously working towards his MBA. It's not every day you meet someone with such drive. That being the case, I thought it would be wise to learn where he got it from, so I called his mother.

Ms. Sharon Davis is quite the spark! A joyful bundle of energy, she's loquacious, vibrant, and optimistic. After speaking with her, it became clear why Jared is the way he is. From day one, she has held Jared and his siblings to the highest standards. A nurse herself, she cared for patients at Johns Hopkins prior to Jared's birth. Each time they returned to visit the area, she would take Jared to the hospitals where she previously worked, and explained the history. Her actions demonstrate the importance of exposure for setting expectations. In order for a child to be capable of achieving something, he or she should first be exposed to it. At the age of three, she bought Jared a Johns Hopkins T-shirt, which served as a constant reminder of a potential future for him.

"At five years old," Ms. Davis told me, "Jared was expected to bring home the paycheck!" Baffled, I had to ask her what that meant. How can a five-year-old bring home a paycheck? "He saw his father and I go to work every day. We explained to him that we went to work, and our reward for doing an excellent job was a paycheck. This paycheck made it possible for us to have a home, buy groceries, and buy a few nice things for him and his siblings. His job was school, and his paycheck was his report card. The same way we expected ourselves to perform well and bring home a check, we expected Jared to work hard in school and get good grades."

What an amazing way to train up a child. From day one, they taught Jared that he was expected to accomplish something meaningful at school, rather than just being present. This allowed him to identify school as something important. He was now able to liken his education to sustainment. *The same way we rely on Mom and Dad to bring home the check so we can eat is the same way I need to bring home my report card. It's important.* An expectation of excellence in academics was set from day one in their household, and it's paying off big time.

Learning with You

Since conducting my survey, I have already begun implementing some of these tactics with my children. My five-year-old now understands the importance of his report card and knows that Daddy will ask him why he didn't score perfectly on everything. Yes, everything. Not some things—everything! In reality, I don't really expect him to do so, but I want him to believe it is possible and for him to set high standards for himself. I want him to bring home the biggest paycheck he can!

You might be thinking, *Now, come on Dr. Dale, that's a bit much. After all, it's just kindergarten. Kindergarten grades really don't mean anything.* But it's not at all about the grades.

Rather, it's about the self-expectations he is developing now and the establishment of habits that lead to excellence. This is the real goal. By themselves, expectations can make someone good. But habits produce greatness. As parents, our goal is to set high expectations that will be transformed into habits.

Another commonality in physicians' upbringing was the expectation to obtain a college degree, and in many homes a professional degree. Growing up, I didn't have the option to not attend college. As a matter of fact, I didn't know that was an option at all. It was simply what people did. I recall my parents saying, "A college degree isn't enough anymore. If you want to be competitive for jobs, you need to get something more than that." Our conversations never focused on if I was going to college and didn't even focus on which college I was going (that never seemed to be very important to my parents). Rather, my parents discussed which professional field I would choose.

I remember one evening when I walked into my parents' bedroom and Papa asked me, "Dale, what do you want to be when you grow up?" I would have been about nine years old at the time.

"I'm not sure," I replied. "I like to argue, so maybe a lawyer."

"That's a good field," he said. "You should also think about being a doctor. But both are great jobs."

On the contrary, I don't ever recall having a conversation about whether or not I wanted to go to college. They had set the stage, so I knew that at minimum, I would be getting a professional degree.

My challenge to you as a parent of a future doctor, lawyer, or professional is to set high and discrete expectations. Write them down and evaluate them at least once per month. When doing this, make sure that you're equipping your children to meet these expectations and fostering their desire to achieve.

PARENT PERSPECTIVE

Imagination Leads to Growth

There is a quote attributed to Socrates that goes: "Education is the kindling of a flame, not the filling of a vessel." I believe this should be a mantra of every parent. I know it was for me raising my three sons, and probably the deciding factor for homeschooling them.

The enthusiasm, creativity and inquisitive spark I enjoyed during my oldest son's early years, sadly diminished as he attended kindergarten and first grade in a traditional public school. I knew in my heart that this curious, questioning and wondering child needed a learning environment beyond a brick and mortar school. Unfortunately, school can be too confining for an inquisitive mind. I wanted more for him and knew there had to be a way to keep his beautiful spark alive. He and his brothers needed the freedom to follow their own interests, ponder their own questions and create their own paths forward.

Realizing this, we became a homeschooling family and created a school as boundless as their imaginations. When a family is not constrained by a school schedule each day begins as an opportunity for discovery. For us, it ranged from raising sheep, to traveling to library programs, to homeschool co-ops, to hours spent creating rocket ships from cardboard boxes and countless hours reading out loud.

There is no greater gift than watching a child discover his or her own "thing" whatever it may be. For my oldest son, it has always been science, for my middle son it was a winding path to physical fitness and personal training, and my youngest son's journey led him to dramatic arts and theater. As a parent, our job is to ground them in the power of their own potential, surround them with love, then sit back and be amazed.

KAREN DOBROGOSZ
Mother of Dr. Aaron Mitchell

6

PROTECT THE ENVIRONMENT

If you want to go fast, go alone;
but if you want to go far, go together.

—African Proverb

"In the beginning God created the heavens and the earth"
(Genesis 1:1 NKJV).

Notice it does not read, "In the beginning God created
man." Have you ever asked yourself why God waited until day
six to make Adam? Just think about it—why would he make
the plants, the land, the sea, and even the beasts before making man? I don't have a definite answer, but I do have my own
suspicion. It seems to me that God, in His infinite brilliance,
thought it was important to establish an ideal environment
before introducing His feature creation, man. His intent was
for humanity to thrive and have dominion over the rest of His
worldly creation. To do this, he placed Adam and Eve in an
environment suitable for their success.

But Adam failed, you say. He sinned!

Well, that's true in a sense, but there's much more to that story, and that's a discussion for another day. However, I think we can all agree that God prepared the environment with care because it was important to Him. Taking a note from His Book, it would be prudent for us to consider the importance of our own environment and that of our children.

Recently I was listening to an interview about juveniles in the detention system. The guest was a director for a rehabilitation center. He expressed his concern regarding the poor behavior of these young individuals and described their efforts to help them rehabilitate. Soon after, the host made a comment and was surprised by the program director's response.

"It's a shame," the host said. "So many people will look at these children and blame their parents. They'll say that these kids must have had a rough childhood or must have been raised in bad environments. That's just not the case."

To host's surprise, the program director interjected to counter the statement. "Actually, a lot of these kids did grow up in bad environments. They did have troubled childhoods. They did have subpar upbringings. We know two things affect behavior: genes and environment. You are born with your genes, and there's not much that can be done about that. Environment, on the other hand, can be modified, and is typically responsible for these children's behaviors."

As a parent, it's important that you do everything within your power to ensure the best possible environment for your children's upbringing.

I'm not going to sugarcoat this; the truth is, environment is everything! Without a suitable one, you will not be successful. I don't mean you *might* not be successful. I mean, you *will not* be successful. If you get nothing else from this book, understand this: you must, and I reiterate, you must, be in the right environment to accomplish your goals.

Yes, it's true that there are countless rags to riches stories in which people came from bad environments. The important thing to realize in these situations is that they *came* from bad environments. They didn't stay there! I know, I'm probably preaching to the choir. If you're reading this book, my assumption is that you appreciate the influence of environment on a child's development. However, because it's that important, we need to spend some time on the topic.

One's environment is the condition in which he or she operates. These conditions are both physical and mental. They're the driving forces necessary for development. In large part, your environment determines your aptitude, your competency, and ultimately your success. Realizing this truth, it's unfortunate that many parents and children were placed in bad environments for reasons beyond their control. Financial recessions, family illnesses, divorce—all these things plague the environments of millions if not billions of people worldwide. It seems quite unfair that some people are dealt a bad hand.

Was it really Chris's fault that he was born to a single mother who was abused by a drug-dealing alcoholic while they lived in the poorest area of town? Probably not. Chris never consented to that. He was put in that environment without being asked. Those were the cards he was dealt, but he can still change his hand. Even better, his parents can make a conscious decision to start changing it for him while he's still young.

Before we delve too deep into the concepts of environment and success, it's important that we understand how researchers study this. In the world of sociology, socioeconomic status is often used as a surrogate for environment. Although there are objections to this approach, we have few, if any, better options.

In accepting this surrogate, the fundamental assumption we make is that individuals within the same socioeconomic class live in similar geographic locations and thus similar environments. This can be supported by surveying educational attainment and median income within various zip codes, counties, or cities. Beyond that, there's also an assumption that those who live in the same geographic environments share similar beliefs and behaviors. Certainly, we know these assumptions fall short of perfect; however, from a practical standpoint, they're extremely useful.

It Starts at Home

America's achievement gap between the "haves" and the "have-nots" begins at a very early age. Many of us believe the myth that the public-school system is to blame for this gap. Certain cohorts of children don't perform as well as others because their schools lack the necessary resources. Media would have you believe that the blame should be placed on other people, outside of the home. *If those teachers only knew what they were doing, then my kid would be doing better. They don't even care about their students.* That's what we're encouraged to think. But is that fair? Furthermore, is it true?

I grew up in Galveston county, which is also where the La Marque school district was located. I say was because in 2015, the Texas Education Agency shut it down due to unmitigated financial and academic problems. This caused the relocation of 2,300 students to another district. As a matter of fact, in Texas, over the past 20 years, five school districts have been closed. In situations such as this, society is quick to point the finger at our educational system. Bad teachers, bad administration, and bad resources. If we could fix these things, everything would be better for our children. Is that really the case? Are the school systems really the cause of lower educational and professional achievement for certain persons and populations?

The reality of the situation is that the schooling a child gets outside of the home is never the primary problem. We've known for decades that the achievement gap begins very early in life. Some suggest that it starts in infancy, from the second a child exits the womb. Others suggest it starts at eighteen months, and still others at three years old. No matter which is most precise, the point stands that achievement gaps begin early. They seed in home environments, not schools.

In 2002, David Burkam and Valerie Lee published a landmark study demonstrating this. Using data from the US Department of Education's Early Childhood Longitudinal Student Kindergarten Cohort, they reported that when students begin kindergarten, the average cognitive score in the highest socioeconomic group is 60 percent higher than that of the lowest socioeconomic group. This is before they even enter the public-school system.

Even more alarming than that cognitive achievement gap are the findings of Dr. Emma Garcia. In 2015, she published, *Inequalities at the Starting Gate*. This amazing 93-page report agreed with prior research pertaining to the achievement gap beginning before kindergarten. What caught my attention, however, was her finding that this gap extends beyond cognitive ability. Noncognitive skills such as persistence, self-control, and attention are also strong predictors of future academic success. Many people, including myself, would argue that the noncognitive skills are more important than the cognitive. It's easier to teach your child to multiply 3 times 5 than to be persistent.

Last week, my wife was examining a nineteen-month-old in her clinic. As she held down this precious child to conduct her exam, he decided that he didn't want to cooperate.

To make that clear, he proceeded to throw a tantrum. That didn't bother Janai. As we say in Texas, it wasn't her first rodeo. We have little ones of our own, and she's done thousands of pediatric exams. What happened next however caught her by complete surprise. This little boy looked straight at my wife and firmly referred to her as a female dog (using a less kind word). Not believing her ears, Janai asked the mother what her son had said. After confirmation of the profane language, Janai asked where the boy learned it from. "He watches his dad and uncle," the mother said. "He got it from them."

This nineteen-month-old child was unable to demonstrate self-control, which is understandable for a child his age. But what's not expected is for him to use a derogatory word in a meaningful negative context. I understand that children have tantrums, mine included, but in this example, poor noncognitive skills are already being imparted in this child's life before he even turns two. Where did he pick it up from? His own house.

I don't mean to pick on this boy and his family. They serve as an illustration to parents that the environment you create in your own home is among the most important determinants of whether or not your child will become a medical doctor—or a lawyer or a software engineer. It starts at birth. The onus to establish an environment for success is on you, not the school system. It's on you, not your pastor. It's on you, not the sports coach. As a parent, you need to build a successful environment for your children. Yes, you read that correctly. *You* need to build it. It certainly won't build itself. Your goal is to make sure your kids have everything they need to thrive socially, physically, and mentally. For this to happen, you must be intentional.

Controlling the Social Environment

Perhaps you've heard it said, "Show me your five closest friends, and I'll tell you who you are. Even better, show me your five closest friends, and I'll tell you where you're going in life." What a powerful and true statement pertaining to social environments. If these five individuals are all millionaires, it's likely that you'll be the sixth millionaire in the group. On the other hand, if these five are drug addicts, there's a good chance you'll be the sixth among them. Friends and family are the center of every individual's environment, including your children's.

Trish Callaway understands the importance of a healthy social environment. Her daughter, Dr. Tiffany Randolph, was my supervising resident when I was an intern physician. During our time in training, Tiffany and I had several discussions pertaining to success, and what it took to become an excellent physician. As a matter of fact, she ended up becoming the vice president for my first company, DiverseMedicine Inc., which ultimately led me to envision and build PreMed STAR (the online community of premedical students). I had always been impressed with Tiffany because she was one of those doctors that could do it all. I don't mean do it all in the hospital—I mean in life. Tiffany was a superstar athlete, an academic erudite, and a talented musician.

Like most parents I surveyed, Trish and Tony Callaway didn't raise Tiffany to become a medical doctor. "It was Tiff's dream since age five," Mrs. Callaway told me during our interview. "One day, back when we lived in upstate New York, Tiff told us she wanted to be a doctor. Then she asked her dad for the name of a good school to go. He told her Harvard. From that point on, Tiffany told everyone she was going to be a Harvard medical doctor. And wouldn't you know it, twenty years later she was a Harvard medical student."

Even as a young child, Tiffany knew what she wanted in life. In the summer, she would lie in the grass for hours cutting leaves, then delicately sow them back together. One day when her father got a large cut on his arm, Tiffany pleaded and pleaded with him to let her stitch it up. She was only five years old! When they told her that he had to go to the hospital so the doctors could suture it closed, she threw a fit and made it known to her parents that she could have saved them the trip had they let her do it.

"I remember how angry Tiff was that day," Mrs. Callaway reminisced. "We didn't want to crush her spirits, so we told her the only reason we went to the hospital was because they had sterile supplies."

Curious to know how they were able to raise such a superstar child, I asked Mrs. Callaway what their secret was. She responded, "We controlled Tiffany's environment and had strict rules about who she could be friends with."

When I heard this, I initially thought it odd. Many parents are ashamed to admit they're controlling, but not Mrs. Callaway. She considered it to be a good thing. "She is my child and I'm responsible for her success," she told me. "If things don't go well, her father and I are the ones liable. So, of course we were controlling."

One of the genius ways in which the Callaways controlled Tiffany's environment was by encouraging her to spend time in their own house rather than going out. "We made sure our house was the place that Tiffany and all of her friends wanted to be. Why go out if you could have more fun at home? Tiffany had the green light to invite her friends over. She knew that the fridge and pantry were always stocked and ready for guests."

In hearing this, I couldn't help but think back to the Garden of Eden. Just like God did for Adam and Eve, they made their home the perfect place for children. This brilliant strategy allowed Mrs. Callaway and her husband to keep a close eye on their daughter, and learn more about her friends. "I wouldn't lurk over them, but if they were in our house, we had a general idea of what they were doing. It was a great way to make sure she had good friends."

Outside of the home, Trish and Tony were just as vigilant. They always knew where Tiffany was and who she was with. "If Tiffany was going out with friends, I'd try to be the one taking them. This wasn't always possible, so if she went out with another parent, we had to know who those people were, or she just couldn't go."

Mrs. Callaway made it clear that there was no negotiating when it came to the people Tiffany affiliated with, and the places she went. "Really we tried to keep her as busy as possible with kids we knew. Tiff has always been a driven person, so challenging her to be the best in the orchestra or whatever sport she was playing consumed her time. If she was doing these things, we hoped she would be surrounded by positive influences."

In the end, for their specific child-rearing experience, Trish and Tony were right to be controlling. From Tiffany's perspective as a child, she thought it was too much, as if her parents went a bit overboard. But today, as a successful cardiologist, wife, and mother, she says, "Now that I'm a parent, I'd say it was appropriate."

Not only did the Callaways appreciate the fact that Tiffany's friends would influence her behavior, but they also understood that the parents of her friends had the same influence. Dr. Holly Shakya demonstrated this in a rather fascinating project. In her publication, she studied the effects of parenting style on adolescent substance abuse. What made this interesting was that she not only tested the effect of the child's parents, but also that of the child's friend's parents. In other words, if you were the child, she wasn't just studying your mom; she also studied the influence that your best friend's mom had on you. Dr. Shakya found that adolescents who had a friend with an authoritative mother were 40 percent less likely to get drunk, 38 percent less likely to binge drink, 39 percent less likely to smoke cigarettes, and 43 percent less likely to use marijuana than the adolescent who had a friend with a neglectful mother. And what's especially interesting about these findings is that they weren't completely a result of how the friend behaved due to the friend's mother's parenting style. Independent of that, the friend's mother's parenting style actually affected the adolescent's behavior. In other words, regardless of how your friends behaved, their moms (or dads) influenced how you behaved. I know this is difficult to understand. Read it again, and it should make more sense the second time around.

With this research in mind, another thing that Mrs. Callaway pointed out pertaining to Tiffany's upbringing was that socioeconomic class was irrelevant when determining who she could associate with. Most of the studies I came across focused on the poor performance of those individuals in lower socioeconomic classes. That being the case, you'd think doctors' parents would rather have their children surrounded by families from higher socioeconomic classes.

This is not necessarily true. The one and only example Mrs. Callaway gave me about guarding Tiffany from certain social influences emphasized protection from affluent individuals. "We were always cautious," she shared. "We had many acquaintances who also had kids around Tiffany's age, but some of them lived in extravagant ways, which we didn't think was right for our daughter. We had to shield her from some of that."

The bottom line here is simple! People are a part of your

child's environment, and as the parent, you must protect your child from negative social influences. Furthermore, you must expose them to the positive influences.

Physician Exposure

In my survey of doctors' parents, nearly half of them, 45 percent to be precise, reported their son or daughter was regularly exposed to a doctor other than their own physicians. This number is significant. These present-day doctors had a vicarious taste of the physician life since childhood. They could see how doctors carried themselves. They witnessed the peculiarities that allowed their physician acquaintances to attain one of the highest social statuses in America. They felt the intangible aura of success. And here's what's interesting about it: it was all subconscious. Most of these now doctors had no idea how impactful that exposure would be.

When I was a boy, Papa would frequently have to run to work while we were out as a family. He'd leave us outside of the hospital saying, "I'm only going to be a few minutes. You all wait right here." I remember sitting in the car, watching as all these men and women walked in and out of the hospital in their long white coats. At the time, I didn't realize it was impacting me, but I now understand that I was being conditioned to view this as the norm. Becoming a medical doctor was never something I believed to be a magnificent feat because I had seen so many of them. Although I didn't know them personally, simply being in their environment made them real.

Reflecting on my childhood exposure to doctors reminds me of a famous Steve Jobs quote.

When you grow up you tend to get told that the world

is the way it is and your life is just to live your life inside the world. Try not to bash into the walls too much. Try to have a nice family life, have fun, save a little money. That's a very limited life. Life can be much broader once you discover one simple fact: Everything around you that you call life was made up by people that were no smarter than you. And you can change it, you can influence it…Once you learn that, you'll never be the same again.

In this quote, Jobs is referring to people's amazement and reverence to technology, architecture, medicine, and other man-made inventions. There is an awe, a certain mysticism that most people have for those who have successfully attained high societal status. That's why men and women faint at the site of celebrities. They treat them as more than human. But those individuals who are constantly around them know that's not true. They know these individuals walk, talk, and sleep like everyone else. Becoming a great doctor isn't a miraculous accomplishment for those who had been exposed to doctors. As a matter of fact, it's an expectation for some people who have physician parents. There's nothing supernatural about it when it becomes part of your natural environment.

While it's not necessary for children to know a physician, I do recommend finding ways to expose your son or daughter to the field. Make it a part of their usual environment in some way. The truth of the matter is there are tons of ways to expose your child to the medical field. It can be as simple as having a church friend who is a physician come over for dinner, or as detailed as enrolling them in a health professions school. As the parent, you should determine the extent of the exposure. The thing that matters however is that they do get that exposure. They need to know that becoming a doctor is possible.

The Physical Environment

An interesting field of study has emerged in recent years. Evidence-based design focuses on strategically optimizing environments to maximize performance. Within the healthcare industry, hospitals and clinics are using this to help their patients heal faster. According to experts in this field, there are five environmental features thought to help patients improve faster: (1) increased connection with nature, (2) patient options and choices, (3) improved social support, (4) decreased environmental stress, and (5) pleasant diversions. As someone who works in hospitals, I can tell you without a doubt that architects and interior designers are building hospitals with these things in mind.

Evidence-based design is growing beyond healthcare settings. Of particular interest, its influence on school architecture is increasing. Some school administrators have attributed decreased disciplinary referrals as well as higher academic performance to evidence-based design in their school infrastructure. Anecdotally, nuances such as more efficient pathways to class, decrease transit times and stress on students. This in turn allows them to perform at higher levels. So, what if you designed your home environment according to the tenets of evidence-based design? If it works for hospitals and schools, why wouldn't it work for your house?

Dr. Dale, do you really expect me to demolish my house and hire an evidence-based architect to redesign it?

Of course not. However, I do expect you to be cognizant of the fact that the physical environment within your house affects the performance of your child. As parents, we are the architects of our homes. It is our duty to ensure everything is kept in order to decrease unnecessary stress and to nurture enrichment. As a child, I failed to understand the importance of this. Papa and MaDear were always breathing down my neck. "Make your bed. Pick up your clothes. Put your plate away."

I couldn't grasp why all these things mattered. Why make my bed if I'm just going to mess it back up tonight? Why pick up my clothes if they're all going into the dirty hamper? At the time, it all felt like unnecessary work. Decades later, I understand the purpose was to maintain an orderly environment, which over the years would allow me to perform well.

Something else I strongly encourage parents to do is have visual cues in the home. These should be cues that constantly trigger your child's mind towards success. For example, in my home office, there are pictures of my boys and me wearing scrubs. Again, I don't necessarily want my children to be doctors, but I do want them to be able to visualize themselves in roles of leadership. They understand what Daddy does for a living and some of the leadership responsibilities that come with it. When they see themselves wearing the same clothes Daddy goes to work in, this stimulates them to ask pertinent questions that are critical for leadership development. And it also generates a sense of pride, which I see in their eyes each time they gaze at the photos.

External cues have played a great role in my successes to date. When I arrived on the beautiful campus at the University of Missouri, I had one thing in mind, and that was to make all A's. At that time, I thought I might want to pursue a career in medicine but wasn't certain. What I was certain about was that good grades provided more opportunity than bad grades regardless of the field of pursuit. So, I made it my goal for the first semester to work hard and get a 4.0 grade point average. It couldn't be that hard, right? With a little encouragement from newly found friends and professors, I'd have the necessary resources and support. Simple, right?

Well, the support part didn't come quite the way I expected. To my surprise, just about everybody I shared my goal with told me that I couldn't do it. As a matter of fact, there was one young lady who would always laugh at me when I shared this with her. She was also a freshman, and I get the sense that she had been jaded by others the same way they tried to jade me.

"Nobody gets a 4.0 their first semester...Good luck with that...Why not aim for a 3.7 the first semester? Just settle in and get used to college."

These are the sorts of things they'd tell us. Every time I saw one of these naysayers, that would trigger doubt in my mind. Simply seeing their faces became an external cue that had been created to destroy my dreams and aspirations. They themselves were not my enemies, but their mindsets were. For me to combat them, I would need reinforcement with my own positive external cues. I had to mold my visual environment into one nurturing of success.

As it turns out, that young lady who was laughing at me actually had a crush on me. I don't know what it was, but she was absolutely infatuated with me. Okay, maybe I was the one who had the big crush, but that's neither here nor there. She'd come over to my dorm room to hang out, and one day I decided to decorate my wall. I took this opportunity to establish my external cues. With her help, my wall became one of pure motivation. Dead center in a large font was a sign that read "4.0." Interspaced between the photos she put up, I added power phrases such as, "Work smarter, not harder. Failure is not an option. Do it for your family."

Every single morning when I woke up, I was forced to face my wall of motivation. There was no escaping it, and in a sense, I had signed a contract with myself to put forth 110 percent towards my goal of a 4.0. When grades came in at the end of the semester, that's exactly what I got. My intentional act to shape my environment with powerful external cues motivated me beyond the words of the naysayers. And that young lady who used to laugh at my goals is now my wife and the mother of my children.

A Mind Is a Terrible Thing to Waste

The mind precedes and supersedes the current reality. Some of you may remember these words: "Butterfly in the sky, I can go twice as high. Take a look. It's in a book. A reading rainbow." These are the lyrics to the classic children's TV show *Reading Rainbow,* hosted and produced by LeVar Burton. I remember the show's opening as if I watched it yesterday. Dragons, spacecrafts, and ships! It was an excellent depiction of how books can take us anywhere. Burton helped to develop a generation of readers. For decades, his entire platform has been to promote childhood literacy. Prior to *Reading Rainbow,* Burton had already starred in the award-winning film *Roots* and *Star Trek.* But rather than continue in these prestigious roles, he opted to promote reading. Others might not have pursued this path, but Burton had a strong why: "I want children to read because I want children to reach their full potential in life."

> *Imagination has a great deal to do with winning.*
>
> —MIKE KRZYZEWSKI,
> DUKE UNIVERSITY BASKETBALL COACH

The mental environment supersedes the physical. As a parent, it's critical that you understand this! Regardless of your socioeconomic status, you have the tools necessary to condition your child's mind for high achievement. No matter the physical circumstances, those of the mental can overcome them. This is the foundation for success. Ask Michael Jordan how he was able to win six NBA championships and he'll tell you it was because of his mentality, not because of his physical ability. The same is true in the field of medicine. Those who make it through the rigorous road and become doctors are able to do so because they have a certain mental environment. One thing most of my physician colleagues have in common is a strong sense of confidence. We know we are capable of doing difficult things. It's not easy to cut open a living human body or to administer medications that could be lethal in the wrong circumstance. But many of us have been conditioned for confidence since our youth.

Throughout my childhood years, my entire family mentally conditioned me for success. When I was in elementary school, my oldest brother, Tony, would tease Daniel and me. As children do, he would say things to insult our intelligence. These were never meant to be harmful; rather, they were to be humorous. I'm not sure why or how this happened, but as an early teenager, Tony realized the importance of the mental environment. He understood that great minds are surrounded by positive thinking, challenges, and encouragement. With this realization, he made the decision that he would only say things to encourage us. Initially, he would still slip and insult us from time to time. "You guys are stupid," he'd jokingly say. However, usually within a matter of seconds he would recant with, "Wait, you know I was just joking. You guys are very intelligent. Extremely smart." He made it a point to actively remind us that we could be anything we wanted to be in life.

Daniel would do the same thing for me pertaining to basketball. Up until college, I was a basketball fanatic. While my friends were out at parties, I spent late nights in the gym. I wanted to be the best, and I thought I was. My coaches clearly disagreed. Year after year something would happen, and I'd get demoted to a lower team or get less playing time than I thought I deserved. But Daniel always encouraged me, telling me I was the best player. "I've seen what you can do, you just need to make sure they see it too," he'd tell me. "Those guys can't guard you!" Even though this had nothing to do with academics, he was conditioning my self-worth. He was shaping my mental environment and in turn my belief system. These encouragements helped to frame a mindset of success, which had a tremendous impact on my performance during my medical training, and even now as I care for critically ill patients.

Time after time I find myself chatting with my premedical mentees about whether or not medicine is right for them. They lack confidence in their abilities. Many of these students doubt themselves even before starting the premed journey. They have a fear of failure that I never had as a premed. From day one, I knew I would perform with excellence. From day one, I knew I would make all A's. There wasn't a single doubt in my mind. And it's not that I thought I was smarter than anybody else, I just knew it was possible and I was capable. I knew this because my family had conditioned my mental environment since childhood. Unfortunately, many of my mentees can't say the same. They haven't been conditioned this way. Although it is possible, and they are capable, they don't realize it.

> *We can't raise our kids to have a growth mindset unless we have a growth mindset ourselves.*
>
> —SUMITHA BHANDARKAR

Promise me this: that you will positively condition your

son or daughter's mind for success. Teach your children to have a growth mindset, to know they can further develop and improve in all aspects of life. Promise me that your physical environment will not limit their mental environment. Promise that you will speak of success in their presence and allow them to see themselves in its light. Encourage your children to read as much as possible. If you can't afford books, go to the library where it's free. Dominating the mind is the beginning of dominating the environment. Teach your child to dominate his or her own mind. This is what doctors' parents do.

Sky's the Limit

Dr. Theodore Nyame is another good friend of mine. Theo is a plastic surgeon who did both his medical school and residency training at Harvard Medical School. He earned his undergraduate degree from Cornell. Not shabby institutions, are they? Your first thought may be that Theo comes from a wealthy family, but nothing could be farther from the truth. Theo spent the early years of his life in a small Ghanaian village, then moved to South Bronx. There was nothing affluent about his family. In his city, the surrounding physical environment was one of break-ins, drugs, and violence. If anybody would have an excuse not to "make it," it would be Theo. But instead, he trained at one of the best plastic surgery programs in the world. How did that happen?

Theo's parents trained him to dominate his mental environment and not be limited by the physical. They used whatever they could to do this. "Dad was a cab driver," Theo shared with me. "Had it not been for him, there's no way I'd be where I am today. He would take my brother and me on drives around New York City and point things out. He'd show us places he aspired for us to be. Hearing it is one thing, but actually getting in the car with your dad and going there is another. Especially when you're coming out of South Bronx. Dad let us know we could become anything we wanted to be, and we believed him."

That's not the only thing the Nyames did for their children. They also set those high expectations, which we discussed earlier. "From day one, they told us the type of education they wanted us to have. Without a doubt, we were going to college but not just any college. They wanted us to attend the best. Harvard, Yale, Columbia, Cornell. It had to be Ivy League." Clearly, this mental conditioning worked. Not only is Theo a Harvard-trained plastic surgeon, but his brother is a neuro-surgeon as well.

PART 3

How to Get In

7

IT'S A NUMBERS GAME

When you have mastered numbers, you will in fact no longer be reading numbers, any more than you read words when reading books. You will be reading meanings.

—W. E. B. DuBois

It's time to get into the nitty gritty. The next few chapters will be pretty detailed. Up until now, my goal has been to provide information that lays a foundation for your child's success. Now I'll tell you what to expect during your child's premedical and medical training. In my Doctors' Parents Survey, over 90 percent of parents reported having some knowledge of what it took to become a physician. Approximately 44 percent reported being extremely knowledgeable. What this should tell you is that if you want your child to pursue a career in medicine, or any profession, it's your duty to learn what it will take for him or her to successfully matriculate into that field. At an early age, it's not the child's responsibility—it's the parent's.

When considering the high percentage of parents who reported having some knowledge of what it would take for their child to become a physician, your first thought might be that they influenced their child to pursue a field they were familiar with. Perhaps there is some truth in that, but keep in mind that the majority of parents said they did not raise their child up to become a doctor. Also keep in mind that over half of those surveyed reported their child was not regularly exposed to a physician other than their family doctor. This suggests that these doctors' parents were proactive, taking it upon themselves to learn about the field and become a resource for their children.

Neither one of my parents is a medical doctor. My mother works in the computer technology industry, and my dad earned his Ph.D. in pathology. Papa worked at a medical school, so he was exposed to the medical school process. Over the years he became extremely knowledgeable about the premedical process as well. I would later find out that he intentionally sat on his institution's medical school admissions committee, in part so he could gain more knowledge and serve as a resource for his children. But what really impressed me about my parents was how much time they spent studying various undergraduate colleges.

Before the internet was mainstream, my folks would go to the bookstore and purchase the annual copies of "top colleges" data books. They would spend countless hours sifting through pages and educating themselves on the process. As I reflect on this, I don't think I ever expressed my gratitude for the energy they put into this. (Thanks, Papa! Thanks, MaDear!) The point I'm trying to get across is that they didn't expect us to figure things out on our own; they were just as much a part of our application process as we were. Could we have figured it all out on our own? Of course, we're all bright individuals. But, there are certainly some jewels that would have been missed without the help of our parents.

This same thing held true when I applied to medical school. Although my parents were not nearly as involved in this application process, they were well versed and had detailed discussions with me pertaining to my decisions. The same held true when I applied to residency, when I applied to fellowship, and even when I was deciding which job to take after I completed my medical training. The entire way through, Papa and MaDear took it upon themselves to familiarize themselves with my current position so they could serve as my counselors. What I learned from that is, at the end of the day, nobody should advise your children better than you. For this to be the case, you must be informed regarding what your children are going through and what they will go through. My job for the remainder of this book is to inform you so you can be your child's best premedical advisor.

Getting into medical school is a numbers game. That's the first thing you need to know. No matter what anybody tells you, please listen to me when I say that numbers matter. While extracurricular activities, past experiences, and recommendations are all very important, ultimately, the student must be able to back all of that up with evidence of academic success or the potential for academic success. His or her GPA (grade point average) and score on the MCAT (Medical College Admissions Test) are the two values used to justify this. Every premed needs to know three numbers: a perfect GPA, the average GPAs for medical school matriculants, and the MCAT for medical school matriculants.

A Perfect GPA

The first is 4.0. A perfect GPA should be the goal each and

every semester. When I speak with my mentees and some tell me their GPA goal for a semester is a 3.7 or even a 3.9. I immediately ask, "Why not a 4.0?" It doesn't make sense to set a goal of missing questions on a test. In effect that's what you're saying when you say your goal is a 3.9 rather than a 4.0. Regardless of if you shoot for the 3.9 or 4.0, you'll be working extremely hard to achieve it, so why not go for the higher score?

So, how can your child make straight A's in college? The full details of this voyage are beyond the scope of this book and can be found in my mentorship book, *Premed Mondays*. I will, however, give you five tips that worked for me during my premedical years.

1. **Sit in the front row of every class.** This was perhaps the biggest key for my academic success in college. Sitting in the front row forced me to be more engaged with the subject matter and also with the professor. This in turn helped professors remember me when the time came to request letters of recommendation for my medical school application.

2. **Attend professor office hours one week before each test.** Professors have office hours for a reason. Unfortunately, not enough students take advantage of them. Many of the premeds that did are now doctors. Even if it's just one concept a student does not understand, he or she should attend office hours to master it.

3. **Network with driven people.** Serious premeds need to surround themselves with people who understand their drive. These people will hold them accountable and encourage them to give it their all. Premeds should take advantage of the PreMedSTAR.com community, where they can network with thousands of like-minded indi-

viduals from across the country, and access numerous resources.

4. **Use tutors.** In addition to attending professor office hours, students should take advantage of resources such as tutors. This is especially true if their campus offers free tutoring. When premeds ask me if they need a tutor, I make it simple for them. If you don't have an A in a class and don't think you can get there on your own, then get a tutor. Tutoring isn't just for students who are failing. Don't let pride prevent you from being the best you can be. There's a reason the top students at America's most prestigious private high schools have tutors. They help them stay on top.

5. **Don't be afraid to appeal grades.** This is especially true for tests that are not multiple choice. Professors are humans too, and they can make mistakes. When we were in college, Janai and I took many of the same courses. I remember one exam in particular, on which I scored significantly higher than she did. When we compared our answers after the test, we saw that many of them were essentially the same, but worded differently. Things like this happen, and it's important for students to know they can challenge test scores. Someone is paying good money for your child's education, so make sure they take the results seriously.

Average GPAs for Medical School Matriculants

I'm aware that not every student will earn a 4.0 in college. That's why it's important to know this second number: the average GPAs for medical school matriculants. I don't want to state an exact number because it changes from year to year, but this information is very easy to find. In the United States, there are three medical school application systems: the American Medical College Application Service (AMCAS), the American Association of Colleges of Osteopathic Medicine Application Service (AACOMAS), and the Texas Medical and Dental School Application Service (TMDSAS). Each of these application services will have its own average GPAs that both you and your child should be aware of.

Although I'm a strong believer that premeds should aim for as high of a grade point average as possible, I also advocate for them to chase their dreams. In my role as a mentor, many students approach me with their academic credentials, then ask if they should apply to medical school. They tell me their GPA, then list off their dream schools. One of the first things I ask is what the average GPAs for those particular schools are. More often than not, they don't know. After we figure it out, I then remind them that this is an average number. That means people with lower GPAs can still get in, and people with higher GPAs can also be turned away. Admittedly, however, when I'm having this conversation, it's usually because the student's GPA isn't great. I then proceed to tell them my wife's story.

Janai is extremely smart, but was a lazy student. She basically slept our entire sophomore year in college and attributed it to catch-up sleep from the prior summer school burnout. Somehow, she still managed to maintain decent grades, but not quite as high as the national medical school matriculant averages. When it came time to apply to medical school, she was told by advisors not to apply because they didn't think she would get in. Janai and I had detailed discussions about whether she should take a gap year and then apply, or pursue alternate healthcare careers.

One day, Janai said, "I'm applying. I'm not going to let anybody tell me no except the medical schools themselves."

Wouldn't you know it—she got accepted into two medical schools and chose to attend Meharry Medical College. My lovely wife would go on to do her residency at the number one family medicine program in the country (at that time).

Let the medical schools tell you no!

This is my wife's message, which I often pass on to premedical students. I must caution, however, that this must be considered within reason. In certain cases, this advice can do much more harm than good, and it would be irresponsible of me to provide poor and unrealistic guidance without that caveat.

The truth is, I appreciate my wife's advisors providing their honest opinion. It is important that we are realistic with students, while at the same time letting them know anything is possible. In reflecting on this, I'm reminded of a speaking engagement I took part in several years ago. I was invited to speak on a panel of leaders in our local healthcare community. During that session, I mentioned that our responsibility as educators, advisors, and mentors is to be informed, then properly convey to students what it takes to get into medical school. If a student appears to have a very slim chance of gaining admission, we must be able to tell them this in a loving manner. Boy oh boy, did that cause a stir among the crowd. I was attacked by a few older doctors.

"You're trying to ruin the hopes and dreams of these students," they told me. But that couldn't be farther from the truth. I'm not writing books and running companies focused on premedical success simply for fun. I want all students to succeed, and yes, a large part of that is providing hope. Hope, however, does not preclude honesty. If a student has a 2.0 GPA, I'm not going to suggest he or she should apply to medical school at that time, unless that student has extraordinary past experiences that will guarantee success. Keep in mind, this is a rather expensive process, both financially and emotionally. It would be cruel and unethical to convey false hope.

I am providing you with these perspectives to illustrate the importance of being an informed advisor. Ultimately, as your child's primary advisor, you should know the average statistics and every possible avenue for them to accomplish their goals. If you don't know these numbers, how will you be able to tell your son whether or not to apply to medical school this year? Or how can you advise your daughter regarding which medical schools to apply to?

Be informed!

Average MCAT Scores for Matriculating Medical Students

The final number you and your future doctor should know is the average MCAT score for matriculating medical students. Know this number for each of the three application services. MCAT is an acronym for the Medical College Admissions Test. This test has been the bane of many candidates' existence, and the great tormentor of thousands if not millions of premedical students. Unless a premed is on a special track (e.g., a guaranteed acceptance program), he or she will be taking the MCAT. Many argue that it's the most difficult exam doctors take throughout their entire careers. Think of it like the ACT/SAT on steroids.

The MCAT is fairly unpopular and carries a bad reputation. Of course, nobody likes a difficult test, but beyond that, it has been criticized pertaining to various biases. The average score for underrepresented minority students is notably lower than that of White and Asian students, yet it is well known that the MCAT doesn't predict what caliber of doctor someone will become.

In 2015, Dr. Aaron Saguil, along with his colleagues, published a study to investigate the association of MCAT scores and future performance. Their study demonstrated that the MCAT is weakly to moderately associated with standardized medical school tests, yet has no significant association or correlation with clinical performance. In other words, their study suggests that the MCAT is an okay exam to determine how well students will test in medical school, but a bad exam to determine how well they will perform as doctors later on.

Partially in an attempt to address this concern, the test has been redesigned multiple times over several decades. Still, the fairness is challenged. During my residency training, I took care of a gentleman who was among those that designed an older version of the MCAT. We had many interesting conversations pertaining to testing, specifically the MCAT. Without hesitation, he told me that he, too, believed the test was biased.

"Yes," he said, "of course the test is biased. So what! Everything in life has some bias to it. There's no getting around it. We just have to find ways to deal with it." It was interesting hearing this from an elderly White man.

I remember thinking long and hard about this before I came to an understanding of his point. As the rules currently stand, the MCAT is part of the game—biased or unbiased. If a student wants to gain admission to medical school, he or she needs to figure out how to deal with this exam.

I'd like to give you firsthand testimony of how to perform extremely well on the MCAT, but I can't do that since my score was average (fortunately, the rest of my medical school application was strong and opened doors for me). So, rather than providing my tips on how to achieve an average MCAT score, I'm going to share five tips from one of my mentees, Megan McLeod, who performed among the top in the country on her exam. Here they are:

1. **Choose the test date wisely.** The MCAT is offered multiple times a year, and students can choose their testing dates. The test date plays a major role in how students prepare. For example, if you choose a date during the semester, you will make a schedule that considers study time for other courses. Some people prefer this, while others would rather take it after a long break to ensure dedicated time for MCAT studying alone.

2. **Strategize a study method and schedule.** This may sound funny, but it's necessary. The MCAT is not a test that people succeed in without a solid study strategy. There is a lot of material covered on this exam, and students need to have a strategy to attack this beast before jumping into the jungle. They must know if they'll take an MCAT prep course, how many hours of studying they'll do each day, which topics to study, when they will take practice tests, etc. It's very important that students have all these things outlined ahead of time!

3. **Take practice tests.** The MCAT is a very long exam with hundreds of questions. A large part of doing well is building up the endurance to complete the test in a reasonable time. To do that, students must practice taking full-length exams. The other major benefit about practicing with full-length exams is this allows the student to evaluate his or her strong and weak areas.

4. **Set goals.** Just like anything in life, having a goal score for the MCAT is crucial for success. Students must know what they are aiming for if they want to hit it. If it so happens that they reach their goal earlier than expected, they can always make the goal a little harder.

5. **Stay healthy.** The MCAT study period is very stressful.

It's very easy to forget about sleep, food, hygiene, etc. Many students complain of weight loss and become ill during this period. This is more likely to happen to students who haven't planned out their study schedule to include time for relaxation and exercise.

Taking the MCAT is like going into the battlefield. Your children need to be well prepared to face that monster. Don't allow them to step foot into the ring without having done their due diligence. Quite a few students have told me they did poorly on the exam because they wanted to see how they would do before deciding whether or not to take a test prep course, or study with a friend. Let me ask you this: Is that a good idea or bad idea?

Bad! Going in unprepared is the absolute wrong thing to do. This test is not easy, and it's not free. Your child needs to come prepared!

In my role with PreMed STAR, I am fortunate to communicate with many medical school recruiters and deans throughout the country. Although it is clear that medical schools are looking for well-rounded candidates, it's just as clear that numbers matter. Here's something I hear often: "Dr. Dale, my GPA and MCAT weren't very good, but the rest of my application is strong. Do you think I'll get into medical school?"

As mentioned earlier, I do my best not to crush dreams while at the same time keeping it real with the students. I tell them the truth. "There are many students out there with strong extracurriculars just like you have, but the difference is, they have the numbers to back it up as well." Students don't need a perfect GPA and perfect MCAT score to get into medical school, but they need reasonable numbers. When advising your future doctor, take heed to the tips in this chapter as well as those in *Premed Mondays*.

PARENT PERSPECTIVE

Being Well-Rounded

My husband, Udom, and I raised Dara and her siblings to focus on achieving their dreams. We taught them to use their daily experiences to learn as much as they could about life, then apply the knowledge to fulfill their dreams. To do this, they had to be well-rounded.

We encouraged our daughters to pursue what they enjoyed. Ima liked dance and tennis. Dara liked gymnastics, track, and cheerleading. Nini liked music, piano and field events. Church and Sunday school were of special importance for all three of them. They fostered mental and spiritual balance, empathy, and generosity. During a church trip, Dara met a teenager with two children. The young girl was in a dumpster looking for food. One of her children had a rash and was scratching insatiably while crying. Dara & her team provided food, but that wasn't enough for my daughter. She was saddened because they had nothing for this child's rash. As we saw her interest in healthcare mature, we wanted to foster it, so we enrolled her in a Certified Nursing Assistant course (CNA) while in high school. This allowed her to spend her summers working in a hospital.

We encouraged Dara to be well-rounded in high school. She participated in track and cheerleading. Cheerleading specifically, helped develop her creativity and leadership skills. She became the head cheerleader for her varsity team and later Rice University's cheerleading squad. Dara was a student

Senator in med school, helped develop a diversity admission program during her medical residency, and led Bible study groups with her church during her pulmonary and critical care fellowship training at UT Southwestern.

Encouraging our three daughters to be well-rounded and pursue what they preferred enabled them to develop confidence, dedication, and good decision-making abilities. Dara is a dedicated physician with good work ethics, cares for her patients, and respects rules and authority. Her life today, in part, has resulted from her implementation of being well-rounded.

ITA & UDOM UFOT
Parents of Dr. Dara Ufot Otu

8

MORE THAN NUMBERS

A good decision is based on knowledge and not on numbers.

—PLATO

Josh has always been a smart guy. From second grade until he graduated high school, he only made one B. He was valedictorian in a graduating class of 1,027 students in a top-rated school district. With stats like that, of course he went on to an Ivy League college. And being a man of intent, when he arrived on his college campus, he knew exactly what he wanted to do with his life: become a medical doctor.

Over the next three years, Josh studied like a mad man. He woke up every day and read for each lecture, ahead of time. Between classes, he flipped through his flashcards, never wasting a minute. In evenings, he reviewed the lecture notes from that day. Josh had a study habit like no other. His grade point average was a 4.0, and he scored in the 99th percentile on the MCAT. When it came time to apply to medical school, everyone knew he was a sure bet!

Then something completely unexpected happened—rejection letter number one came. A few days later, the second came, then the third, and so on. As smart as he was, Josh did not get into medical school that year. What happened?

Josh made the cardinal mistake of thinking brains alone are sufficient. He failed to understand that doctors are more than numbers, and because that's true, premedical students must also be more than numbers. Throughout his journey, everyone from his parents to his advisors had been so enthralled with his intellect that they overlooked his poor interpersonal skills, his lack of nonscholastic achievement, and his overconfidence. They all fell into the trap of thinking the smart guys and gals always win. They equated merit with numerical scores, failing to appreciate that there is much more to success than what can be objectively measured. Thankfully for patients, medical school admission committees are mindful of this truth, and they look beyond the numbers.

This story about Josh isn't about a particular person. Any medical school dean of admissions will likely tell you a very similar story. The point parents and students must understand is that the days of purely objective data are long gone. The kid with the highest numbers is no longer the obvious winner. Don't misunderstand what I am saying; numbers do matter, but there's much more to it than that!

As a parent, you should be aware of what medical schools are looking for in an applicant. It's easy to fall into the trap of simply pushing your child to get the best grades and ignore other important pieces to the puzzle. There are a variety of extracurricular activities that are essential to matriculation. The premedical landscape is hypercompetitive, and many students silo themselves off to focus on outperforming others. Not only can this lead to rejection letter after rejection letter, as in Josh's case, but it can also lead to unnecessary stress, anxiety, and depression. Knowing this, be sure to counsel your future doctor on issues pertaining to healthy social interactions and fostering growth in humanity.

The more important thing about extracurricular activities, however, is that they expose students to life. This exposure provides invaluable learning opportunities, which will allow your child to develop in ways the classroom simply can't offer. I know many doctors whom I would choose over other doctors who graduated at the top of their class. The reason I would choose these individuals is because they've had real-life experiences in which they needed to work with teams and innovate to solve problems. They've learned from the classroom of life. Textbooks aren't very good at teaching those kinds of things.

> *If life is a classroom, then I am one of its most ardent students.*
>
> —ROSALIND BREWER, COO OF STARBUCKS

Before we jump into various extracurricular activities, which are popular among premeds, we should touch on one thing that many medical school admission committee members consider above all else: *letters of recommendation.*

Letters of Recommendation

A good word from a highly respected person carries a lot of weight, perhaps even more than grades and MCAT scores. For various reasons, many premedical students struggle to obtain excellent (not just good) letters of recommendation. And here's the thing: A student with a perfect application may only need mediocre recommendations. But one great rec letter from the right person can be the thing that sets the average premed apart from the crowd. There are a few things you should know which will help your future doctor get excellent rec letters.

The most important factor in getting excellent recommendations is *relationship building*. Time after time, premedical students approach me complaining that they don't have anybody to write them a rec letter. This complaint is often associated with an excuse of some sort. "My classes are too big to connect with the professor," or, "I was busy with a full-time job and couldn't build a relationship." This might be okay one or two years prior to the application process, but it's not okay one or two months prior. My question to them is, "What on earth have you been doing these past few years?" Unfortunately for these students, either nobody told them to start building relationships on day one, or they didn't comprehend the importance of doing so.

From the moment I set foot on the University of Missouri's campus, I knew I had to build a strong network. An especially important part of this network would be the various professors and other faculty/staff who would contribute to my education during those undergraduate years. I used a variety of tactics to ensure my professors knew who I was. The front row middle seat was mine. Every single lecture, you knew where you'd find Dale sitting. And every so often (maybe every second or third lecture), I'd raise my hand to ask a question, simply to make sure the instructor knew I was paying attention. Perhaps most importantly, one week prior to each exam, you could find me sitting in office hours, one-on-one with the professor. After all of that, do you think my professors knew who I was? They most certainly did! Not only did these strategies help me to get wonderful grades, but they helped me to get some of the best rec letters those professors had ever written.

Notice I am repeatedly using adjectives that suggest phenomenal rec letters. Most students get good letters of recommendation from their writers. That being the case, good then becomes average. Great then becomes good. But excellent remains excellent. When admission committee members read rec letters, they understand the code of the letter writers. They know if a professor really thought the student was amazing or if they are simply placating one of the many premeds who needs a letter to apply. The latter doesn't bode well for the applicant. It might be good enough to get the student accepted, but then again, it might not. If your future doctor's application isn't otherwise flawless, he or she needs to focus on getting outstanding rec letters.

Extracurricular Activities

Okay, so you've got the grades, MCAT score, and rec letter portions down. What else could there be? Isn't that enough to get students into medical school? Nope, not at all. Here's where things get interesting! Your child must learn to excel in extracurricular (EC) activities. If I wrote a book called *How to Raise a Doctor* without reviewing extracurricular activities, albeit in brief, I'd be doing you a disservice.

Research

Let's begin with research. This is a contentious topic for premedical students because they feel they must do research to get into medical school, yet some of them don't like it. Medical schools gain reputation and rank by publishing scientific knowledge; therefore, they want scientists. That being the case, there is a push to begin training these future researchers while they are still in the premedical phase of their careers.

More importantly, getting exposed to research at an early stage helps many people decide which path to take. I have quite a few friends who loved the idea of research much more than they loved the idea of patient care. So they pursued their Ph.D. rather than the MD path, which I chose. Had they not participated in undergraduate research, they may never have found their true passion. Many students, however, don't enjoy conducting research. To be precise, they don't like basic scientific research, which involves spending a good amount of your time in a laboratory. It takes a certain level of patience and curiosity to conduct research, and if you don't have it, time spent in a lab could feel like torture.

I joined Dr. Troy Zars's research lab my second semester in college. We did memory and learning work with *Drosophila melanogaster* (fruit flies). I truly enjoyed those days. Janai also did research, but worked in Dr. Joel Maruniak's lab, directly across the hall from where I was. One of her favorite stories to tell happened early in my fruit fly days. I was fresh on the job and extremely excited. Half of that excitement was really nervousness. Dr. Zars had already trained me on the basics to get things up and running, including how to handle the flies.

With my relatively new girlfriend by my side, I set up my microscope and grabbed a vile full of uniquely bred flies. After sedating them, I gently poured the flies onto the pad so I could evaluate them under the microscope. Things started off smooth. Then, in my periphery, I saw a fly buzz away. Seconds later, I saw another fly off, and then another. Soon after, I was swarmed by an air force of fruit flies in full combat mode.

Mind you, I was new to the job and thought these were an expensive, hard-to-breed, genetically unique type of fruit flies. Accordingly, I couldn't lose a single one of these little guys; if I did, I was sure Dr. Zars would fire me. So, I did what any future doctor would have done in that situation—I began swiping my arms in a desperate attempt to capture each fly one by one. Janai stood behind me laughing, and possibly wondering if she needed to get a new boyfriend. Needless to say, I was unable to capture those flies, but I did learn soon after that we had an entire stock of them. Furthermore, we could breed them with very little difficulty and produce ten times as many.

When I think back to my lab days, the memories are fond, but for some premeds, the lab is like a jail cell. The issue arises when students force themselves to do research simply because they think it will help them stand out as a premedical student. Some advocate for this approach. They contend that students who dislike research should pursue it anyway for the sake of their medical school application. I disagree. People don't perform at their best when they don't enjoy the task. In such situations, the student does a subpar job and, in the process, wastes a lot of peoples' time and resources. Most importantly, they waste their own time.

It would be much more beneficial for your individual growth and edification to find something you enjoy than to spend the time to master it. Being a concert pianist is more impressive to most admission committee members than conducting research at an average level. Students should not take part in an extracurricular activity simply to check off a box from the premed list. Even when shadowing physicians, they shouldn't do it unless it interests them. Please don't misunderstand what I am saying. I don't mean that you should only do the things in life that make you happy, but in the premed world, it's easy to be pressured down a path that might leave you unfulfilled. So, my final take on research is that premedical students should give it a shot. They won't know if they like it until they try it. After trying it out, they can then decide whether or not it's for them.

A common question pertaining to research is whether it's better to have multiple projects that span a period of time, or one long project. Neither situation is necessarily better. The false assumption in this question is that the longer a premed spent on a project, the more committed he or she was. But what if that student spent four years working on a project that others could have completed in four months? On the contrary, that might suggest the student was not dedicated to the completion of the project. What really matters is the depth of understanding, and the results of the project. By results, I'm not referring to the actual data and conclusions; I mean how the student grew and personally developed from conducting the research. I'm talking about personal results.

Medical school is tough, and those sitting on admission committees want to be certain a candidate can see something through to the end with proper understanding. They need to know a candidate can handle the heat and won't quit. That's what the rigor of medical school boils down to!

Clubs and Organizations

Moving on from research, there are several types of extracurricular activities that all premedical students should take part in. One of these is membership in clubs and organizations. Being an active member of a club is an indicator that you can contribute positively to a team. Medicine is a team sport. In the ICU, I treat all sorts of conditions that require me to call upon my team: nurses, respiratory therapists, social workers, physical therapists, dieticians, radiology technicians, chaplains, physician colleagues, etc. There is no way I can run an effective intensive care unit without these people by my side. That's what premedical clubs are about—accomplishing goals as a team.

A common pitfall for premedical students is when they are members of many clubs, but are not active in them. Club activities should be meaningful in the same way research experiences are. It's not the number of clubs joined that matters; rather, it's all about how the student contributes and adds value to those clubs. Being the president of one very active club is more impressive than being a bystander in ten clubs.

Regarding which clubs to join, your future doctor should be an active member in whatever organizations he or she finds interesting. If it's arts and crafts, then I suggest joining that club and climbing the ranks into a leadership position. If martial arts really get your child going, then getting involved with a martial arts club would make sense for him or her. I do, however, recommend that all premedical students be a part of at least one premedical club. This is critical because it gives them the network to obtain important information that otherwise might be hard to come by. For example, if there will be a speaker from the local medical school's admission committee, that information might be limited to the premed club that invited the speaker. These clubs are a key source of information that no premed should miss out on.

Clinical Exposure

The other extracurricular activity that all premeds must take part in is obtaining clinical exposure. Obviously, students who claim that medicine is the right field for them should be able to show they have spent adequate time in clinical environments to be certain. Medicine isn't for the faint at heart, and anybody who commits to this profession needs to know what it's really about.

I can't tell you how many people I've met over the years who were premed until they saw someone else's blood for the first time. That's kind of important to know, wouldn't you say? Don't apply to medical school if you can't stand the sight of blood. How do you learn whether or not you can tolerate blood? By getting into a medical setting and looking at blood!

I am amazed when some premedical students speak to me with so much confidence pertaining to their future career, yet have little to no clinical experience. This extracurricular activity is non-negotiable; students must do it.

There are a variety of ways to gain clinical exposure. The classic way is to *shadow a physician*. The student somehow connects with a doctor, then sets a date and time to follow him or her during the workday. Although it sounds relatively straightforward, there are some pearls of wisdom that your child should know. Shadowing experiences can be difficult to come by. Earlier in the book, I briefly outlined how to go about securing such opportunities. The bottom line is that sometimes students must take a risk, put themselves out there, and be prepared to deal with rejection. Doctors are busy people, and shadowing is additive work for them. When they say no, it's not personal.

One of the best things a premedical student can do to increase the chances of getting a shadowing opportunity is to limit the time to two hours maximum. The longer students are there, the more teaching the doctors must do. This results in them getting home to see their own families later than usual. When it's a choice between a premedical stranger and one's own family, who do you think wins? But if the student lets the doctor know ahead of time that he or she is only looking to see a couple of patients, that doesn't sound bad at all. Most doctors would be glad to accommodate that.

Securing the shadowing opportunity is just the first part. After showing up for that shadowing day, the student needs to be fairly invisible until given the green light. By this, I mean asking questions during down times and not while the doctor is with a patient, speaking with another health professional, writing prescriptions, or writing notes. The student must find the balance between appearing interested and not being bothersome. This is how to score a second date! But remember, you can't get the next date unless you ask. So, at some point during that interaction, the student needs to say something along the lines of, "Thank you so much, Dr. [Name], for letting me come in and shadow you today. This was great, and I took some good notes. I hope I didn't slow you down too much."

At this point the doctor will reply to the effect of, "Not at all, come back anytime." That response is simply reflexive. How do I know you ask? Because I've used it, and it's been used on me. It works! However, if for some reason the doctor doesn't make the offer, then the student should be more direct and ask, "Would it be okay if I reach out to your assistant and find another time to shadow that works for you in the future?" Most of the time, the answer will be yes. The biggest hurdle with shadowing is getting a foot in the door. After that, securing future shadowing opportunities becomes much easier.

With all that said, I was a premed at one point and have mentored enough to know that it's not that easy to find a physician to shadow. So, what can premeds do if they cannot find a doctor willing to take them on? My first recommendation in such a situation is for that student to *find a clinician extender to shadow*. By clinician extender, I am mostly referring to physician assistants (PAs) or nurse practitioners (NPs). Premedical students don't take advantage of these shadowing opportunities as much as they should. Most clinical experiences will be similar whether your child follows an actual physician or a clinician extender. In both instances, patients will be seen, test results will be interpreted, and notes will be written. The key difference is the extra discourse that happens between the doctor and student, which can shed more light on the actual physician lifestyle.

Shadowing clinician extenders in and of itself is a great clinical experience. Beyond that, it's a wonderful way for premeds to get a foot in the door. Typically, where there are PAs or

NPs, there will also be MDs or DOs. In many environments, these clinician extenders work side by side with supervising doctors. Just by being there, students increase their chances of getting closer to physicians they otherwise couldn't reach. The student now has a clear path to walk right up to the doctor and request a shadowing "date."

I want to be clear, however, that it's inappropriate to shadow a clinician extender solely for the purpose of getting closer to the doctor. That would be like going out with a girl just to score a date with her best friend. When shadowing a PA or NP, the student should use that experience to learn more about patient care and what clinicians do. Furthermore, this is the perfect opportunity to explore the PA or NP career as an option. The truth of the matter is that many individuals would prefer that career path, but they don't know very much about it. Some students don't even know it exists. I recommend that every premed shadow NPs or PAs at least once to gain this experience and pick their brains. You never know, this might be the right career for your child.

Another way to get shadowing experience that many pre-meds don't consider is by *shadowing resident or fellow physicians*. Residents are fresh out of medical school, and fellows aren't too far ahead of them. Oftentimes, these young doctors are zealous for their field and anxious to share knowledge, as well as their experience, with the next generation. Medical school admission committee members don't necessarily care what level physician premeds shadow. What's more important is that the student has an adequate amount of clinical exposure, which allows them to understand the career ahead. It has been my experience that resident physicians are typically excited and honored when premeds ask to shadow them. I've even seen situations in which premeds shadow medical students. At the end of the day, your student has to find a way to get in the door. Getting past the bouncer is the hard part, but once you're in the party, as long as you behave, nobody is looking to throw you out.

Work Experience

The next type of extracurricular activity that all premeds must consider is work experience. For some of you parents, hearing the words work or job for your college kid is daunting. School is tough enough as it is, and now they're expected to work too? Well, I wouldn't necessarily say they're expected to work, but I will say that a lot of premeds I know work or worked. Thinking back to my premed days, pretty much all of my now-doctor friends had some sort of job. Regardless of how much money their parents had, they worked. So what's the catch? How can students be expected to get the grades, do the research, lead the clubs, shadow clinicians, and work on top of all that?

The most important thing pertaining to working is that students must choose the right type of job. The goal here is to kill two birds with one stone. For example, remember I told you I did research throughout my undergraduate years? Well, that was paid research. It was a job. And in that situation, I actually killed four birds with one stone. I did research, worked, formed a relationship for a strong rec letter from a professor, and learned more about genetics (which helped me with my coursework). There's nothing quite like getting paid to do the things you're supposed to be doing anyway! Other than research, premed job favorites include library staff, dorm hall coordinator, campus mentor, campus tutor, phlebotomist, and scribe.

I want to take a moment to highlight the scribe job. During my premed years, this wasn't nearly as popular as it is now. Had I known about it then, it's likely I would have applied for a position. Scribes are note takers for doctors and other clinicians. Most of the time, you'll see them in emergency rooms, but other departments can use scribes too. This is an awesome job and is another one that kills four birds with one stone. As a scribe, the premed gets paid, acquires clinical experience, forms a relationship with a potential rec letter writer, and learns things pertinent to their education. I strongly encourage premedical students to pursue this option if possible.

The other important thing to be mindful of when considering employment for premedical students is that summers are golden. There are tons of summer opportunities specifically for premedical students that pay good money. After my first year of college, I did research at MD Anderson Cancer Center in Houston, Texas, that summer. This came with a nice stipend of a few thousand dollars. My second summer was spent doing an enrichment program at Yale University School of Medicine. This one came with a stipend of a few hundred dollars, but all accommodations and food were covered. My third summer was spent conducting research at Harvard Medical School, and this also came with a stipend of a few thousand dollars.

Many parents want their kids to come home for the summer. This is a reasonable desire, and as a parent, I cannot argue against it. But as a physician who last spent the summer with his parents at age eighteen, I understand the value of getting away from the nest to start working seriously towards a career. Moms and dads, please listen to me. You must let them go and let them grow! My summers were invaluable in my premedical maturation process and just as invaluable in gaining me admission to medical school.

A common scenario is as follows. Ashley just finished her freshman year of college and has no summer plans. Mom and Dad run a local bakery shop and could use an extra set of hands, so they ask her to work for them during her time off. Ashley spends the summer kneading dough and ringing up customers at the cash register. Let me first state that there is absolutely nothing wrong with this situation. Working for the family business and gaining real-world experience is excellent. That being said, I believe the real-world experience is just as useful for the premedical student when there is a clear correlation between the job role and life as a physician. It's likely that Ashley could have made a similar amount of money (if not more) doing something medically oriented instead of kneading dough. Also, Mom and Dad could have hired someone else to do that job for the same price they paid Ashley. The sacrifice, however, would be the time spent with family.

This summer job scenario highlights another common mistake students make: not planning for upcoming breaks. As parent and chief advisor of your future doctor, it's your responsibility to ensure their days are well accounted for. One of the more frustrating situations I encounter as a mentor is when summer approaches and my mentee has no plans. This is something that needs to be addressed six months in advance. Many summer opportunities have application deadlines early in the winter semester. In the case above, Ashley should not have waited until summer to know what she'd be doing.

Ultimately, medical schools are looking for intelligent problem solvers who work well in a team environment. This is what doctors are. Your child's GPA and MCAT score are only part of the criteria. The student who has a great life story, who thrives in extracurricular activities, and has a respectable MCAT score and GPA is the type of student that medical schools are looking to admit.

PARENT PERSPECTIVE

Making Great Choices

My oldest daughter, Joy, is an anesthesiologist and critical care intensivist. My second daughter received her MBA from Harvard Business School and is working in consulting. My son is a successful entrepreneur. My husband and I are first-generation immigrants from Taiwan. We did not raise our children with the "tiger mom" philosophy, as many Asian parents from my generation did. Even though many Asian parents want their children to become doctors due to the prestige, we did not tell my oldest to become a doctor. In fact, we didn't know she wanted to be a doctor until her freshman year of college. I raised her to be able to make her own choices and also to be responsible for them.

One of these choices was how to spend money. I gave each of my children an allowance; I think it was $100 a month back then. Instead of telling them how many times they could go out to eat or go to the movies, they made their own choices about how and when to spend their money. If they chose to eat the inexpensive school lunch, then I paid for it. If they wanted to buy fast food or go somewhere with their friends, it would come out of their allowance. This taught them how to budget money, be resourceful, and make tough decisions. All of these are important life skills.

Though I trusted my children to make many decisions, they still had strict rules to follow. Starting from elementary school, we had a rule that there was no watching TV from

Sunday night through Thursday night. I made this rule so that my children would have to do their homework instead of procrastinating. Beginning in high school, my daughter had a strict curfew and was not allowed to spend the night at anyone's house. This helped her avoid compromising and potentially dangerous situations. Also, I did not allow my daughter to wear makeup or painted nails to school, so she would be more focused on her studies than her appearance. Finally, my children were required to attend Sunday school and Chinese school. This gave them a strong community of friends and a strong cultural identity.

Most important though, my husband and I always tried to show our support to our children. My oldest daughter, the doctor, was a competitive gymnast. Even though we sometimes thought her many hours of training and out of town competitions took time away from her studies, my husband attended every competition and videotaped each one of her routines. We always encouraged her to pursue her interests and passions.

MARIA CHEN
Mother of Dr. Joy Chen

9

COUNT THE COST

"Suppose one of you wants to build a tower. He will first sit down and estimate the cost to see whether he has enough money to finish it, won't he?"

—Jesus Christ

"On the first day of Christmas, my true love gave to me: a partridge in a pear tree. On the second day of Christmas, my true love gave to me: two turtle doves and a partridge in a pear tree." Most of you are familiar with those first two stanzas of *The Twelve Days of Christmas,* a classic carol. Have you ever considered how much money the singer's true love spent that Christmas? Sure, the items are sweet and the concept is cute, but that's one extreme Christmas budget! I recently read a *Business Insider* article by Akin Oyedele, who pointed out that the cost of the items on the list totaled approximately $34,000. Oyedele astutely recognized something else about this true love's expenditure. With the exception of the twelve drummers, all the items were purchased more than once. The result is a whopping $156,000 dollars!

Just imagine you were the true love. Day one, a partridge in a pear tree. That's okay, I can afford that. By day four, things are starting to add up, but you're deeply in love and want to be sure your spouse knows it. By day eight, you're in too deep to stop and you have to go to the bank to take out a loan. By day twelve, you're filing for bankruptcy. Yep, that's what applying to medical school is like. Okay, maybe it's not quite that bad, but the point I'm making is you need to count the cost ahead of time, or else you'll run up a tab like the song writer's true love.

Everybody knows that medical school tuition is expensive, but what many people don't realize is that the medical school application process is also expensive. This being the case, parents should be aware of the financial commitment that's necessary even before starting medical school. The last thing you want is for application season to come around, only to find out that your child isn't prepared to apply due to limited resources. And just to make it clear, we aren't talking pennies. Consider the fact that some students open a new line of credit just for the medical school application process. Let's break things down a bit.

MCAT Prep Courses and Fees

The cost of undergraduate education, room and board, etc. is a given. Most people know what they're getting into with all of that. The surprise costs typically don't show up until it's time to prepare for the MCAT. It's likely that when this time comes, your student will come to you with a question, "Mom, Dad, should I take an MCAT prep course?" The reflex answer is an obvious yes. By and large, it is accepted that good MCAT prep courses improve test scores. Appreciating this truth, you respond, "Yes, how much does it cost?" What you hear next will surprise many of you: $1,000, $2,000, $5,000, $9,000. This is the general price range of the various MCAT prep courses, depending on the level of intensity and resources allocated to a student. Unfortunately, for many families, the cost of the prep course is near prohibitive.

Some students try to save money by studying for the MCAT without enrolling in a prep course. Many of them are successful, but many of them are not. Those who aren't often regret that decision. I have also seen a combination of the two. Another common scenario in my world as a mentor is as follows: John has a decent GPA and is confident he is a strong premedical student. He's got the grades and extracurricular activities. Everybody knows that John is a sure bet, including John himself. So, he decides not to enroll in a test prep course because he knows he'll ace the MCAT the same way he did his coursework. This way he can save the money and use it for applications. John gets to studying and does so for four months. Test day comes around, and he bombs it!

I'm not writing this to endorse any specific test prep company, but I must shed light on this topic as I have seen so many students make huge mistakes in handling this. First things first: premeds don't have to take test prep courses to ace the MCAT. As mentioned earlier, some will self-study and score among the nation's best. The key is knowing if you're capable of doing that, ahead of time. Notice in the prior scenario, I didn't mention anything about John taking the time to see if he was prepared to go at it alone. Before making the decision whether or not to invest in a test prep course, every student should take a practice exam and see how well they score. They should also use that exam to identify their weak areas. This will help determine if they can improve on these areas alone or if they need extra help. Parents, educators, friends, please listen to me! One of the best pieces of MCAT advice you can give to a premed is to *have them take a practice exam before they delve deep into studying.*

Okay, so let's say John did take the practice test at the start of his studying and did horrible. Does that mean he needs to enroll in a prep course? Not necessarily. My recommendation is that premeds take their practice test early enough so they can then do a trial of self-study. Three to four weeks of self-study followed by a second practice test should be sufficient to gauge how effective the study strategy is, thereby allowing them to know at this time whether or not to call in the pros. Keep in mind, however, that many people recommend studying for the MCAT for a total of four to six months (depending on the intensity level of the student's study). This is important to remember because you don't want your student to get stuck in a perpetual self-study trial period.

Here's what you as the chief advisor of a premedical student need to understand: *Organized test prep courses really can improve scores.* You should be involved in the decision-making process pertaining to whether your child enrolls in a course or not. Know your child's practice score, and know the average scores for her schools of interest. The MCAT is the make or break point for so many students! If your premed isn't getting the scores needed for admission, strongly consider making the investment to hire a professional who will help him increase those scores. Also keep in mind that there are various fee assistance programs to help students afford MCAT test prep courses. For the parent who is reading this book and has a pre-law or pre-nursing student, for example, the same is true in many of those fields. Don't disregard the test prep option because you think it will cost too much. Be resourceful, or better yet, have your student be resourceful to find ways to bring the cost down.

Okay, we've talked enough about MCAT prep courses. Let's not forget about the actual test. At the time of me writing this book, the costs of the MCAT exam is $310. I know, that doesn't sound like much after hearing how about the prep courses, but it's not a trivial amount. The MCAT is offered multiple times a year and can usually be found in cities near college campuses. This is nice because there are typically no travel or accommodation costs associated with this exam. Also, the Association of American Medical Colleges does have a fee assistance program for the MCAT exam.

Application Fees

We must make sure that people who have the grades,
the desire and the will, but not the money,
can still get the best education possible.

—BARACK OBAMA

The actual cost to apply to medical school is highly variable. Of course, the most important factor is *how many schools a student chooses to apply to.* At the time of this book, the average number of schools a premedical student applies to is approximately 15. Among the three medical school application services, AMCAS is currently the largest. It serves as the primary application system for the majority of medical schools in the United States. I recommend that you refer to their website for up to date application fees. The following information was obtained from there. Today, as I am writing this book, when John applies to medical school via AMCAS, he will pay $160 for the first application he submits, then $39 for each subsequent application. In the case of a student who applies to fifteen medical schools via AMCAS, the cost is $706.

So what happens after he has submitted his primary applications? Typically, there is a short (or long) period of anxiety, then the secondary application requests start coming in from the medical schools he applied to. Secondary applications are specific to each school, and their basic purpose is to help admission committee members decide if the applicant is a good fit for the school's mission. For example, if my school focuses on rural healthcare and your application clearly states you want to work in a large city, then we don't have a love connection there.

In our hypothetical situation, John receives secondary application requests from 10 of the 15 schools and decides to submit all 10. Again, according to the AAMC, secondary application fees usually range from $0 to $150. We'll take the average and assume a cost of $75 per school that John is applying to. That's another $750! At this point you might be thinking, *Wow, are we done yet?* No, we're not. It's time for the interview process.

John did an excellent job connecting with each school's mission and ended up getting seven interviews. He's determined to become a medical doctor and refuses to take any chances. That being the case, John accepts every interview offered to him. The economics of travel are highly variable. For four of his interviews, John flew and stayed in hotels. For the remainder he drove and stayed with friends. Conservatively, we can estimate this interview process including a suit, transportation, accommodations, and food to have cost John $2,000. Again, that is a very conservative estimate. *Now are we done?* No!

John gets accepted into three medical schools and is ecstatic. Some students actually go out for a "second look" to see the school again so they can make a final decision. John feels confident that he knows where he wants to go, therefore he forgoes the second-look invitations. Finally, to wrap up his application process, John pays his dream school $100 for the pre-enrollment deposit. Now, we are done (until the actual medical school tuition kicks in). At the end of it all, John spent $3,556 dollars to apply to medical school. If we add the cost of the MCAT exam to that, he spent $3,866. This is what you should expect when it's time for your child to apply to medical school. Oh, and don't forget to throw in the cost of an MCAT prep course, if applicable.

Final Caveats regarding Finances

One thing I must caution you against is letting your student start off on the wrong foot pertaining to credit. I am fully aware that there are many families who cannot afford these costs; therefore, the applicant will have to use credit cards to finance this entire process. I cannot stress enough the importance of sound financial guidance during this process. The last thing you want is for your child's credit to be ruined before medical school even begins. If you are not savvy in areas of finance, be sure to find the resources necessary to ensure your student makes wise credit decisions during the application cycle.

Don't lose faith. Yes, the process is expensive, and it might break the bank, but there are a few things to keep in mind. First, there are resources out there to ease the financial burden. For example, as mentioned earlier, the AAMC offers a fee assistance program that can reduce the cost of the MCAT as well as primary medical school application fees. Furthermore, some medical schools waive their secondary application costs for qualifying students. This is just one example of a resource that your child might be able to capitalize on. Also keep in mind that there are tons of scholarships just waiting to be applied for. Have your student search for, and apply to, as many of these as possible. This can make all the difference once medical school begins! The second thing for you to keep in mind is that this application process should be viewed as an investment. Here's a personal illustration along those lines.

When Janai and I were applying for residency, we flew out to North Carolina for her UNC interview and my Duke interview. We had booked a hotel online via Expedia. When we arrived in town and drove to our hotel, it was rundown. If I had to guess, I'd say it was a two-star at best. If possible, the hotel industry may have given it a negative rating. My lovely wife didn't want to stay there, and I couldn't blame her.

When we went to cancel our reservation, we learned that she had booked the hotel in a certain way, which turned out to be nonrefundable. At the time, we were newlyweds and had very little money to our names. We ended up losing that $200, and that was a large percentage of our bank account. To say the least, I was frustrated at her. Had I been alone, I would have stayed in the hotel, but I couldn't do that with her since she was clearly uncomfortable.

"Dale," she said, "why are you mad? In a few years, you won't even remember this two hundred dollars!" Her words resonated with me, and I came to realize that at the end of the day, it's best to do things right. Making sure my wife was comfortable was the right thing to do, even though it hurt our wallets.

Assuming your child is a solid premed, the same goes for the application process. Although you may be putting down $4,000, if your child is admitted to medical school, the return on investment will be well worth it. Like Janai said, sometime in your near future, that money will be a distant memory.

PARENT PERSPECTIVE

Advocating for Your Child

I want to encourage you along this journey of child-rearing. When you love your child and fight for their success, anything is possible. I learned that from my parents, who left elementary school to work during the great depression. They fought for their eight children to graduate high school. And now, my daughter is the first doctor in our family.

The journey hasn't been easy, but it's been worth it. As a Mexican-American who lived through the segregation and discrimination of the 1960s, I was determined to ensure my children had the same opportunities as every other child. When I enrolled Erica in a public middle school that would not allow her to join the gifted program, I met with several administrators and received excuses and conflicting information. I knew she was smart, so I persisted until she was tested for the program. Erica then became one of the few underrepresented minorities in the program.

In writing this, I'm reminded of a time when Erica wanted to enroll in a clinical shadowing course that would require us to purchase a car. Finances were limited, but we did what we had to do for her to succeed. My husband and I did without, and I worked cleaning a house. We've always raised our children with the Christian value of loving your neighbor as yourself, and I knew our sacrifices were worth it when Erica began giving rides to help her neighborhood friends.

Help your child blossom and instill greatness into their life.

Read to your child daily as their young minds are developing. Turn off the television and spend time with them. Expose them to the arts and music. Be present in their lives and always let them know they are worth fighting for.

My most humble prayers for you and your children.

DEBBIE OROZCO SOLÍS
Mother of Dr. Erica L. Solís

Conclusion

FIGHT FOR YOUR CHILD'S SUCCESS

Is it a crime to fight for what is mine?
—TUPAC SHAKUR

Just last week, we were out at a lovely family event. It was a wonderful setting with food, face painting, and balloon animals. Kids were running, jumping, laughing, and dancing. It truly was a good time. After we finished dinner, my wife got up and took the kids around to partake in the fun. I sat down and chatted with a friend for about thirty minutes before I got up to join my family. When I caught up with Tony and Jace, they had been standing in line to have a balloon animal made. Actually, they wanted balloon swords so they could fight against Daddy at bedtime. So I stood there with the boys for five to ten minutes, watching them play with other kids while waiting in line. At some point, I stepped away to make a call.

Approximately ten minutes later, Janai walks outside carrying our daughter with Tony and Jace hysterically crying as they followed their mother in a duckling pattern. These weren't fake cries. They were the uncontrollably snotty cries. As a father, one thing I don't do is play with my boys' emotions. I take their feelings very serious and am keenly aware of their "my feelings have been hurt" cry. That's what this one was.

I rushed off the phone, concerned for my boys. "What happened?" I asked.

"They said we were out of line, but we weren't," Tony replied through his sobby snorts.

The boys didn't have their balloon swords, and I was curious to know why. "Where are your balloons?"

This time Janai answered for them. "The gentleman making them said they were out of line, and they had to go to the back if they wanted their balloons."

Tony spoke up. "We were not out of line."

An awesome thing about being a parent is you really get to know your kids' characters. At this stage in his life, Tony basically never lies. He is very straightforward, to the point that people might think he is being rude and talking back. The interesting reality, however, is that Tony is very concerned about the truth. Anytime he hears something that he doesn't believe to be accurate, or if he is accused of something, he appropriately offers a statement of correction. This was one of those moments, and I knew he was being honest. Besides, I had already stood with him and his brother in line for several minutes, watching all the kids play together. Nobody was really in line. They were standing in line the way you'd expect three to seven-year-old children to stand.

But Dr. Dale, you say, it's just a little balloon. Who cares? Why not just stop by the store and get him some placation ice cream on the way home?

Nope, I couldn't do that. As a father, I had to make a decision that had larger implications. My boys were pridefully hurt, which perhaps is the worst type to be. Furthermore, as a Black father of two Black boys, I had to consider what this would do for their future interactions. This is the part that my wife couldn't appreciate at the time. She was able to walk them out of the event without realizing the ultimate implications, because it's not part of her everyday life to consider such things.

"Come on," I told my boys. "Let's go get your balloons. You stood in that line for forty-five minutes like every other child. I even stood next to you and watched as other children patted your heads, pushed you, and shifted in and out of line. You're going to get your balloons just like they did."

By now you should understand that I couldn't care less about the actual balloons. My mission was to restore the pride of my boys and ensure they did not lose an ounce of self-worth. When we got back inside, my suspicion was confirmed. Tony continued to cry and suddenly became fearful as he stepped to the back of the line. This behavior was very unusual of my son. By this time, there were only two or three people ahead of him because the event was concluding.

He said, "Daddy, I don't want a balloon anymore."

I asked him what he meant by that and why. A few minutes earlier he had been crying because he wanted one.

"I just don't want one anymore, Daddy. Can we go home?"

I told him no, that we were going to get him and Jace their balloons like everyone else.

"But, Daddy, I just want to go home. I really don't want it anymore."

Again, I reiterated my plan, and he understood that it wasn't going to change.

"Daddy," he said, "can you stand in line with me?"

This nearly broke my heart. It was now clear as a crystal that my boy had taken a direct blow to his confidence and was scared of the man making the balloons. Again, this was very out of character for Tony, who never needs me to stand with him in line.

I sat down in a seat next to the short line. "I'm right here, Son."

He pulled my arm. "No, Daddy, but can you stand with me when we get to the front of the line?"

I nodded, verbally confirmed, then did as promised. Jace and Tony got their sword balloons, and I offered to pay the gentleman a tip for staying a little later than he was scheduled. I know this fine balloon artist did not mean to hurt their feelings, and probably had no idea what was going on.

My number one job as Tony, Jace, and Mavyn's dad is to fight for their success in all aspects of life. I hope that as parents you understand why the balloon incident was of critical importance. Although my children are young, I've had to stand up for them in similar ways on multiple occasions. I'm emphasizing this concept because I've witnessed situations in which other parents were unable to, or unaware that they should, stand up for their children. The only reason I can do it is because it was modeled for me as a child. Had it not been for my parents interceding in similar ways, there's no way I'd be a medical doctor today.

Papa Comes to the Rescue

One example of my parents' intervention occurred when I was in the sixth grade. We were sitting in class bored when my teacher stepped out into the hallway. A buddy and I were play-fighting, as was common among kids our age. He and I had been friends since the third grade, and there was never any animosity between us. But our teacher didn't agree. She walked right in the middle of our pretend fight and reprimanded me. Not him, just me. Next thing I know, I was under investigation by the principal's office and facing several threats of discipline. The accusation brought against me by the teacher, not my buddy, was "attempting to choke another student." Thank God, He gave me parents who knew their son well, and who knew to fight for him.

I should make it clear that I wasn't a bad kid. I never got into real trouble, didn't use vulgar language, and never got into drugs. Pretty much all I did was go to school and play ball. Sure, I could be a little loud depending on the class, and perhaps had issues with speaking out of turn, but I was never a troublemaker. Yet, for reasons unknown to me, I was repeatedly subject to poor conduct accusations. I remember Papa going to my school on various occasions to meet with the leadership. I never asked him what happened during those conversations, but I do know he defended his son like no other. Whatever he did, it worked. That teacher who accused me of choking another student subsequently apologized, and for the remainder of the school year, she treated me like a teacher's pet.

> *A child needs to know there's always someone who can give them the love and care they need.*
>
> —LA JUNE MONTGOMERY TABORN,
> CEO OF THE KELLOG FOUNDATION

At the time, I didn't grasp what had happened. It's probably best I didn't, because I would have been jaded towards the teacher. It wasn't until twenty-one years later at Papa's sixtieth birthday party that it dawned on me. My siblings and I took to the microphone to say some words about him. When it was my turn, my reflections led me to those situations when he and MaDear came to my rescue. While speaking about Papa, I completely lost my composure and broke down in tears. For the first time, now that I had children of my own, I understood what he and MaDear had to do during those years to fight for our success.

I knew without a doubt that if they had done what so many other parents often do—simply let it go, or fail to fight with fervor—I would have never excelled academically. It's likely I would have been marked as a problem child, and this rumor would have spread from teacher to teacher. As a result, my reputation would have been tainted. Teachers would have treated me in a different way, and I would have lost confidence in my academic prowess. I've seen this happen time after time to students at various levels of training. My parents saved me from that outcome. As a child, I couldn't express it, but I knew this to be true. The confidence gained by seeing your parents put their necks on the line to protect you is unparalleled.

MaDear Protects Her Cub

One weekend when I was about nine years old, MaDear took me to a soccer game. My friend Jarrod came along with us. While waiting for my game, we were off playing, and another child (whom we had never met) called us niggers. We ended up getting into an argument, and the boy's mother joined in to defend her son. MaDear quickly arrived on the scene, and after we explained what happened, she defended us like a lioness protecting her cubs. My cute little mother who couldn't hurt a fly was ready to put on her gloves and jump in the ring. Just witnessing her readiness to get in the fight on our behalf empowered me to take on the world.

Knowing your parents love you and believe in you that much makes it possible to soar. If you take nothing else from this book, take this: fight for your child's success! Get in the battle with your children. Make sure they know you're right there with them. When opposing forces come, they need to believe you will take up arms and stand by their side. There are very few things parents can do that are more important than this.

The constant theme among the parents I interviewed is that at some point, they figured out what their children should become, then they did what they could to bring it to fruition. They did not force them to become doctors, but rather suggested the option and ushered them to success. It's true that they all raised doctors, but more importantly, they trained leaders. That is what I plan to do, and what I want you to do as well. I don't know whether or not my children will become doctors, but I do know that I will apply the principles I have learned from those who raised doctors, as a means of ensuring my sons and daughter become leaders in whichever careers they pursue.

My hope for you as a parent is that my writings have provided valuable insight, not just pertaining to how to raise a doctor, but how to raise a leader. Again, as a young dad, I am on this journey with many of you. My boys have made it clear to me that they have no interest in pursuing medicine, and I have no intent on forcing this upon them. I will provide them with the information necessary for them to make their own decisions. My goal is not for them to wear the white coat. My goal is for them to positively impact lives regardless of what career they choose.

I conclude this book on a personal note of faith. I firmly believe in the God of the Bible, and that He guides us along every journey. In my short time as a parent, I've realized that this isn't an easy gig. At times, we face challenges that seem insurmountable, but we must remember that the Lord is watching over us.

To the young mother who reached out to me on behalf of her son, may God continue to watch over you. Thank you for being the lioness in your child's life. Fight for your children's success! Be a prayer warrior, waking up every day to ask for personal guidance, as you guide your children. My prayer for you, and for every parent reading this book, is that the good Lord grants you many successes as you raise not just tomorrow's doctors, but tomorrow's leaders. In the mighty name of Jesus, Amen.

A VERY SPECIAL THANK YOU!

Training to become a doctor is extremely rewarding. Along the journey, you form lifelong relationships. When I committed to write this book, I reached out to many of my physician friends, and they graciously assisted me by connecting me with their parents. From the bottom of my heart, I am beyond grateful for your help, and even more grateful to call you friend. It goes without saying that I could not have written this book without you.

And to the parents of my physician friends, this book is your wisdom! Thank you for sharing it. Thank you for changing lives! Thank you for giving kids a shot at becoming doctors. Thank you for making proud parents. You don't know how many lives will be positively impacted because of your contribution. It has been an honor for me to serve with you in this capacity. On behalf of every person who will benefit from this book, thank you!

Gratefully yours,

Dale Okorodudu, MD

Faith. Family. Friends.

MEET DR. DALE

Dale Okorodudu, MD is a husband, dad, and physician. He is the author of *Premed Mondays* and the founder of PreMed STAR. Dr. Dale's passion lies in developing the physician leaders of tomorrow.

To learn more about Dr. Dale,
visit **www.DoctorDaleMD.com**.

Attention Premedical Students!

Be sure to join the online community for premedical students. Download the app for free in your app store. With PreMed STAR, you can network with other pre-meds, manage your resume/curriculum vitae, share class notes, get recruited by participating medical schools, and much more.

www.PreMedSTAR.com

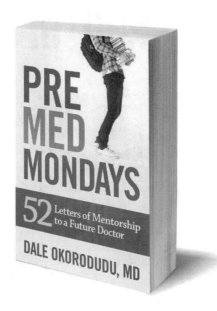

SEND ME YOUR PHOTO!

Thank you for reading my book! I pray it has transformed you in some way for the better. If it did, here's how you can let me know. Take a nice photo (it's ok to get creative) and send it to me with a brief statement of how this book has impacted you. I'll be sharing these photos on my website and social media platforms, so we can support each other in developing tomorrow's leaders in medicine.

Email the photo and your social media
names to me at:

Dale@DoctorDaleMD.com

Again, thank you so very much for reading my book!

www.facebook.com/DoctorDaleMD

www.twitter.com/DoctorDaleMD

www.DoctorDaleMD.com